W9-CTB-171

Flowers at My Feet

Western Wildflowers in Legend, Literature and Lore

Brenan M. Simpson

hancock

house

ISBN 0-88839-394-2
Copyright © 1996 Brenan Simpson

Cataloging in Publication Data
Simpson, Brenan, 1933–
    Flowers at my feet

    ISBN 0-88839-394-2

    1. Wild flowers—Canada, Western—Miscellanea. 2. Wild
    flowers in literature. I. Title.
QK203.W47S55 1996   582.13'09712   C96-910397-2

All rights reserved. No part of this publication may be reproduced, stored in
a retrieval system or transmitted, in any form or by any means, electronic,
mechanical, photocopying, recording, or otherwise, without the prior
written permission of Hancock House Publishers.
Printed in Canada

Editing: Colin Lamont and Nancy Miller
Production: Lorna Brown and Nancy Miller
Cover Photos: Brenan Simpson

Illustration Sources:
James Anderson. *Trees, Shrubs, Food, Medicinal and Poisonous Plants.*
B.C. Department of Education. 1925.
Nathaniel Lord Britten and Addison Brown. *An Illustrated Flora of the
Northern United States, Canada and the British Possessions.* 1913.
W. H. Fitch. *Illustrations of British Flora.* 1924.
Gerard's *Herbal, or General Historie of Plantes.* London, 1597.
Rev. C. A. Johns. *Flowers of the Field.* 1905.
Various Nineteenth-Century Nursery Catalogs

Published simultaneously in Canada and the United States by

HANCOCK HOUSE PUBLISHERS LTD.
19313 Zero Avenue, Surrey, BC V4P 1M7
(604) 538-1114   Fax (604) 538-2262
HANCOCK HOUSE PUBLISHERS
1431 Harrison Avenue, Blaine, WA 98230-5005
(604) 538-1114   Fax (604) 538-2262

Flowers at My Feet

CE 2   8.50

Dedicated to Ann, Catie and Kirstie.

Contents

Introduction

I cannot see what flowers are at my feet,
Nor what soft incense hangs upon the boughs,
But, in embalmed darkness, guess each sweet
Wherewith the seasonable month endows
The grass, the thicket, and the fruit-tree wild;
White hawthorn, and the pastoral eglantine;
Fast-fading violets cover'd up in leaves;
And mid-May's eldest child
The coming musk-rose, full of dewy wine,
The murmurous haunt of flies on summer-eves.
John Keats, Ode to a Nightingale

John Keats may have chosen to stumble around in the dark, listening for his nightingale, tramping on flower beds and bumping into trees, but most of those who study nature prefer to do so on a warm summer's afternoon, when they can see quite clearly the flowers at their feet, the trees above their heads and such other "perils and dangers of the night" as the 1662 edition of *The Book of Common Prayer* of the Church of England entreated against.

My wife and I go for a walk nearly every day on the island where we live. Between our house and the local store, a distance of somewhat over a mile, I can think, without straining my brain too much, of at least seventy-five different wildflowers which we see, growing by the road side, during one season of the year or another.

We live on a B.C. island in the Strait of Georgia. From the hill behind our house, we can see on a clear day, a ring of mountains all around us. In the north lies Mount Garibaldi and the Coast Mountains of British Columbia. To the east are Mount Baker and the Cascades. The Olympic Mountains of Washington State form our southern horizon and the mountainous spine of Vancouver Island completes the circle in the west. Inside the bowl formed by these ranges lies what is sometimes called the Georgia Basin, consisting of Georgia Strait and Puget Sound. Rising from the waters of the basin are the Gulf Islands of Canada and the San Juan Islands of the United States, separated only by a line drawn on a map by Kaiser Wilhelm of Germany in 1872.

It is on these islands and the large expanse of coastal land surrounding the basin that all of the wildflowers in this book, and many more, live and flourish. A number of them, of course, grow elsewhere too, on this continent and even further afield. Some arrived here as seeds, in hay used as packaging material in the crates of possessions of the early settlers. Some seeds fell in the droppings of birds, migrating north or south along the Pacific Flyway. Some escaped from gardens and became settlers themselves and some, since packages of wildflower seeds have become commonplace in garden centers and nursery catalogs, have been scattered deliberately to hide the scars of development or to create wildflower gardens where nature managed quite well before.

> All sorts of flowers, the which on earth do spring,
> In goodly colours, gloriously arrayed.

as Edmund Spencer put it about 400 years ago.

I am not a botanist, so there is no complex scientific material in this book. It is a mixture of the language, lore, legend and literature, having to do with some of our local wildflowers.

Most of the contents of this volume first appeared in the columns of the *Island Tides* newspaper, which serves the southern Gulf Islands. I would like to thank the editors of that paper, Christa Grace Warwick and Patrick Brown, for putting up with these ramblings for more than three years and even giving them space. I also wish to thank Helen and John O'Brian of Pender Island and Vancouver for their encouragement and assistance in developing the material into book form. And, of course, my appreciation also goes to my wife of thirty-eight years, Ann, who keeps me walking around the island, even on cold and wet winter days, so that we can continue to see the flowers at our feet.

The Book of Maccabees in the Bible says, "It is a foolish thing to make a long prologue and to be short in the story itself."

I hope that this prologue has been short enough.

9

HUCKLEBERRIES

Whan she homward cam, she wolde bringe wortes and othere herbes.

Chaucer, The Clerk's Tale

Human beings have long recognized a connection between greenness and life. Every spring they saw the apparently dead fields and trees turn green as they came to life again and people reflected this knowledge in the words which they used.

In Latin, the source of much of the English which we speak today, the word *viridis* meant green, *virens* meant alive, *virga* was a twig and *virgo* a young woman. The root of these words, 'vir,' has given the French word *vert*, meaning green and our English words, verdant and virile. It also gave us one of our Old English words for a plant, *wyrt*, which was used in the *Vespasian Psalter*, written around 825 A.D.

By the time Chaucer was writing his *Canterbury Tales* in about 1390, a *wyrt* had become a 'wort,' as in the quotation at the top of this page, and in that form it has come down to us unchanged as part of the common names of several plants, including the St. John's wort, which grows wild all over this area.

A little wyrt was a 'wyrtil,' and in time, the little red berries which grew on one particular wyrtil became known as 'wyrtil-beryes.' Later on, because there were no dictionaries in those days and everyone spelled words in the way that they pronounced them, the letter H crept in and produced a 'whyrtil-berye.' In some parts of England, this evolved into a 'hurtil-berye' and it was that form of the word that crossed the Atlantic with settlers to the New World during the sixteenth century. By 1634, in a book called *New England's Prospects*, it had become the 'hurtleberry.'

Just south of New England lay the Dutch colony of New Netherland, which the English captured in 1664, renaming it New York, and imposing a new official language on the inhabitants. The Dutch, however, seem to have had some difficulty pronouncing hurtleberries and the best that they could come up with was 'huckleberries.' The word appeared in a description of New York, written in 1670 by David Denton. Whether it became a local joke or just an easier word to say, it quickly caught on throughout the thirteen colonies and, of course, remains the name of the plant to this day.

In England, however, the whyrtil-berye evolved into a 'whortleberry,' which is still its common name, and that's why Mark Twain never wrote *Whortleberry Finn*.

The red huckleberry, *Vaccinium parvifolium*, grows throughout North America, including our area and is so well known that it needs no description here. *Parvifolium* means small-leaved, which it is. As for *Vaccinium*, think of Dr. Edward Jenner, an English physician who, in 1796, noticed that milkmaids never seemed to have the pock-marked faces which resulted from smallpox. He felt that there must be something in cows' bodies which gave these women immunity from this often fatal disease. He tried out his theory by scratching the skin of an eight-year-old boy, James Phipps, and rubbing into the wound an extract made from a cow's body fluids. Although the rest of the Phipps family were affected by smallpox, young James didn't catch it.

From the Latin word for cow, *vacca*, Jenner produced the name of his new treatment, 'vaccination,' and a huckleberry is a *Vaccinium* because cows like to eat it.

PERIWINKLE

Scots, wha hae wi' Wallace bled,
Scots, wham Bruce has aften led,
Welcome to your gory bed,
Or to Victorie.
Robert Burns, Bruce's March to Bannockburn.

They were an untrustworthy lot, those Englishmen. Late in the afternoon of June 18, 1306, Robert the Bruce, King of Scots, surrounded the city of Perth with his Scottish army and called upon the occupying English garrison to come out and fight.

The English commander refused. The day was too far gone for a proper fight, he said. He'd come out in the morning and they'd have all day for a good battle.

Bruce agreed, set a time to meet the next day, backed off his troops and saw them fed and bedded down for the night. But while they slept, the English stormed out from the city gates and charged the unprepared Scots. Bruce's army was shattered and among those captured by the English was one of the Scottish Commanders, Sir Simon Fraser, a name familiar in this part of the world.

A ballad called *The Execution of Sir S. Fraser*, published in England later that year, tells the rest of the story:

> Y fettered were ys legges
> Under ys horse wombe.
> A garland of peruenke
> Set upon ys hede.

So what does that mean? Well, in earlier times, in many parts of Europe, garlands of periwinkle (peruenke) were placed on the heads of prisoners being led to their execution. That is probably where the Italian name for this plant, *fiore di morte* or flower of death, originated.

There is a famous phrase attributed to Julius Caesar, "I came, I saw, I conquered," or in Caesar's own words, "*Veni, vidi, vici*." There is a bit of a dispute as to whether Romans pronounced the letter V as we do or whether they pronounced it as a W. This argument has been going on for centuries and one of its results was the wyrt not being a 'vyrt' and English people not eating 'vortleberries.' Those who support the W-sound theory pronounce Caesar's words as "waynee, weedy, weeky" (or even weechy).

Anyway, *vinca* is the past tense of the verb *vincere*, meaning to conquer or overpower. So a person who is overpowered and, as the custom was in those days, pretty sure to be killed, is in that unfortunate situation '*per*' (through) being *vinca* (conquered). If one puts these words together and pronounces the V as a W, one ends up with a 'perwinca', so it's not too hard to see where the name periwinkle came from, and *pervinca* was the name given to this same plant in a book written by another Roman, Pliny the Elder, who lived just a few years after Julius Caesar.

When the botanic name was assigned to periwinkle, however, the per part was dropped and the plant became just a *Vinca*, the larger of the two forms which exist being the *Vinca major* and the smaller, logically enough, being called the *Vinca minor*. Both of these plants are actually European natives and have been brought here by immigrants. Both have their place in herbal medicine, being prescribed to stop bleeding, reduce blood pressure and as a general tonic. A close relative from Africa, the Madagascar periwinkle, is an important source of a drug used in the treatment of some forms of leukemia.

But back to the battle outside Perth. Bruce himself escaped, reorganized his army and went on to drive the English invaders out of Scotland at the Battle of Bannockburn on June 24, 1314.

Scots form the third largest ethnic group in Canada, and if Quebec should ever separate Scots will form the second largest group. Should that come about, I believe that the name of June 24 ought to be changed from St. Jean Batiste Day as it is at present to Bannockburn Day.

All those in favor say "Aye."

ELDER

There were three children from the land of Israel,
Shadrach, Meshach, Abednego.
They took a trip to the land of Babylon,
Shadrach, Meshach, Abednego.

Spiritual, recorded by Louis Armstrong in 1938

"Nebuchadnezzar was the King of Babylon," the song goes on to say and the Book of Daniel in the Bible says so too. In a little bit of bad luck for the trio of Jewish tourists, Nebuchadnezzar had decided at that time to build a golden statue and order everybody to worship it by falling flat on their faces whenever a fanfare was played by a band consisting, in the King James version of the Old Testament, of a "cornet, flute, harp, sackbut, psaltery and dulcimer." The penalty for failing to do so was to be thrown into "the burning, fiery furnace."

Shadrach and his friends refused to worship this Babylonian god and suffered the prescribed consequences.

Perhaps it's a bit of a quibble, but, in fact, the sackbut shouldn't have been in that band, for it hadn't been invented in Nebuchadnezzar's time. The translators who produced this version of the Bible ought to have paid more attention to an earlier translation by John Wyclif in the 1380s. That version listed the instruments too, but instead of a sackbut, it had a sambuke and a sambuke is definitely not a sackbut. To be technical, a sackbut was an early form of our modern trombone, while a sambuke was a small, stringed instrument, rather like a lyre. But it differed from the lyre by having a high-pitched sound, which came from the particular type of wood used for the frame. The wood came from the hollow branches of the elder. And the old Latin name for the elder, which continues on now as the botanic name, was *Sambucus*. Which name came first, the tree's or the instrument's, is anybody's guess.

Of the several varieties of elder in the world, the one which grows wild around here is the red-fruited elder, the *Sambucus racemosa arborescens*. Usually, as will be mentioned later on in this book, a botanic name consists of only two words, but occasionally, as in this instance, a third word may be added to differentiate the plant more accurately. Most elders are shrubs, but this one is more of a tree and *arborescens*, which means treelike was added to the name so as not to confuse this

14

particular variety with the others. The word *racemosa* means that the flowers hang down in bunches, each little blossom at the end of a tiny stalk, in what are known to botanists as racemes. The common name, red-fruited elder, also distinguishes this variety from other elders, which generally produce black or dark blue berries.

Elder Tree

Our local elder grows to a height of up to fifteen feet, with leaves which John Gerard, an English herbalist described in 1597 as consisting of "five or six particular ones fastened to one ribbe...nicked in the edges and of a rank and stinking smell." He did concede, however, that the little white flowers which appear in May, have a sweet scent.

Throughout history, the elder has been associated with magic and religion. Freyja, Scandinavian goddess of love, lived in an elder tree. Possibly this tradition, passed on by invading Vikings, was the origin of the old superstition in England that, before cutting a branch from an elder, one should kneel down, remove one's hat and ask with respect, "Give me some of thy wood and I will give thee some of mine, when it grows in the forest." If no reply came from the tree, it was alright to take a branch or two, but history doesn't record what happened to those who failed to keep their promise to replace the wood later.

Elder flowers and berries are still used in medicines and cosmetics. The Italian liqueur, Sambuca, is made from the berries and so is a very good country wine. Small boys make pea-shooters and whistles from the stems, which are easy to hollow out by poking out the soft pith in the middle. Elderberry tea is made from the dried berries, which also form part of the recipe for a Chateauneuf-du-Pape wine. And if one does not want to go to the effort of any of these, the elder makes a beautiful garden specimen.

So what happened to Shadrach, Meshach and Abednego? God saved them from dying in the burning, fiery furnace and Nebuchadnezzar was so impressed by this, that he destroyed his golden image, converted to Judaism and told his people to stop falling on their faces every time they heard the sound of the sambuke.

15

GERANIUMS

It's no go the picture palace, it's no go the stadium,
It's no go the country cot with a pot of pink geraniums,
It's no go the government grants, it's no go the elections,
Sit on your arse for fifty years and hang your hat on a pension.
Louis MacNeice—Bagpipe music.

Those of us who have failed to make it to Hollywood, the Rose Bowl or
the Senate may well console ourselves, particularly if we are fortunate
enough to live on the Islands, that we have at least achieved the country
cottage with a pot of pink geraniums.

Having said that, I'm sorry to be about to burst the bubble. The reality
of the matter is that the chances of there being geraniums in the pot
are fairly minimal and what are probably in there are pelargoniums.

To be fair, they do belong to the same plant family, which comprises the
geranium, commonly called the crane's bill, the pelargonium or stork's
bill, and the erodium or heron's bill. All of this 'bill' business, comes
from perceived similarity between the seeds of the various plants and
the bills of the different birds. But the main practical difference between geraniums and pelargoniums is that the former are native to the
temperate northern hemisphere, whereas the latter come mainly from
South Africa, where it is much warmer, and freeze to death if they are
left outside in our winters.

If you want to see a true geranium, probably all that you will have to
do is look around in your gardens, for at least two varieties grow wild
abundantly in this area and a few others appear more rarely. The most
common is the *Geranium molle*, or dove's foot geranium. This is a very
early flowering annual plant, which continues to bloom late into the
year. It has a tight rosette of grayish green leaves, which are about an
inch wide, fairly circular in shape and have ruffled edges. Its flowers are
pink with five petals regularly spaced, each with a deep notch at the top.
So if there is something like this growing in the grass, it's most likely
to be this geranium.

The second most common local family member is herb Robert, the
Geranium robertianum, which used to be considered an important medicinal herb in the Middle Ages in the treatment of wounds. It is
thought to be named after Robert of Moleme, an eleventh-century

healer, who presumably used it extensively enough to get his name attached to it. This is also an annual plant, but it prefers to be in a more shady location than the dove's foot. It is also taller, with very deeply indented leaf edges and has thin purple stripes on its pink petals. Its strongest recognition features however, are its red stems and its slightly unpleasant smell.

Doves-foot

The first known reference to herb Robert comes in a manuscript written in 1265, in which it was called 'Herba Roberti.' A volume on herbs, published in 1578 states that "the fourth kind of geranium is known in English as Herbe Robert," so even back then they knew what a geranium was. And it couldn't have been a pelargonium, because they were only discovered by Europeans when John Tradescant brought some back from the Cape of Good Hope in about 1660.

There's still time to get a government grant, if you're lucky, but if that fails, my advice would be to do as Mr. MacNeice suggested. Put a pelargonium in your pot and hang your hat on a pension.

CAMAS

The Chief made a present of two half-dried salmon and about half a bushel of roots of two kinds; the one called Ka-mass a white root of a slight bitter taste which becomes a favorite and is agreeable to the stomach;...

David Thompson, Travels in Western North America 1784-1812

Some of you must have read *Breaking Smith's Quarter Horse* by Paul St. Pierre, or seen the movie version starring Glen Ford, which came out in the 1970s. There was also a version produced by the Canadian Broadcasting Corporation as part of the *Caribou Country* series, back in the old black and white days and that's the version which I remember best, one scene in particular.

At the Courthouse in Williams Lake, Gabriel Jimmyboy is on trial for murder. A very old native Indian, Ol' Antoine, played by Chief Dan George, is in the witness box to speak for his young friend. Ol' Antoine claims to have been with the Nez Percé people in Montana back in 1877, after they had been driven off their land by the U.S. Army and were trying to escape into Canada, like the Sioux under Sitting Bull had done before them.

Ol' Antonine stands there in the box. "I remember that day," he says. "All around us in them snow hills is the white soldiers.... Chief Joseph waits for us on saddle horses. I am tired of fighting," he said. "All the old chiefs have been killed by the white savages.... The peoples are cold and we have no blankets.... The peoples are hungry and there is no more meat."

The sad truth is that Chief Joseph was real and what he said was fact. The Nez Percé territory was in the Snake River area of eastern Washington, where Washington, Oregon and Idaho all come together. The Lewis and Clark expedition had passed through there in 1806 and Captain Lewis had written in his diary while he was there that "the Quawmash is now in bloom...It resembles lakes of fine, clear water."

The Quawmash or camas bulb had been one of the main sources of food

18

for the Nez Percé people since time immemorial and the great abundance of the plant in that area was the reason why they had settled there.

The Nez Percé were not a warlike people. When they saw what civilized whites like Captains Lewis and Clark had to offer, they sent back east to St. Louis for books and teachers. What they got instead were missionaries who encouraged settlers to follow them and the gold-seekers were not far behind. The settlers cheated the Natives out of their land and let their herds of pigs root in the prairies where the camas grew, destroying the bulbs and depriving the Nez Percé of their basic food supply. When some of them rebelled under the leadership of Chief Joseph, the U.S. government sent in 580 soldiers, commanded by the one-armed General Oliver Otis Howard to suppress them. Some of the Nez Percé tried to flee into Canada, but so many of them died in the snow or from the sabres and bullets of the U.S. Cavalry that Chief Joseph had to surrender. "The peoples are hungry and there is no more meat." And all they had wanted was to save their camas bulbs.

Two varieties of camas grow in the Pacific Northwest. The early camas, *Camassia quamash*, grows to about a foot tall and its spikes of blue flowers open in April and early May. There's also the great camas, *Camassia leichtlinii*, named after German botanist Max Leichtlin, which can reach over four feet tall. Both of these have whitish flowered versions, which are fairly uncommon and there is another white-flowered relative, the *Zygadenus elegans* or death camas, which is highly poisonous and which the Nez Percé tried to eradicate from among the edible varieties, so that they would not be dug and eaten by mistake.

An Irish-born artist, Paul Kane, visited Vancouver Island in the 1850s and later wrote a book about his travels. In it he said, "Fort Victoria stands upon the banks of an inlet.... Its Indian name is the Esquimelt, or place for gathering Camas, great quantities of that vegetable being found in the neighbourhood."

He was wrong then about the meaning of Esquimelt and he would be wrong now about the great quantities of camas. Settlers and developers have had their way and "there is no more meat."

19

VIOLETS

A violet by a mossy stone,
Half hidden from the eye;
Fair as a star, when only one
Is shining in the sky,
William Wordsworth, She Dwelt among the Untrodden Ways

It might well have been our own bright star-yellow local violet that Wordsworth was talking about. Its common name is the evergreen violet, because in this climate its leaves stay green all winter, but by the time one speaks about a yellow evergreen violet, the combination of colors can lead to a state of complete mental confusion. Its botanic name is *Viola sempervirens. Sempervirens* means always alive or, by implication, forever green, and as for *Viola*, Greek mythology tells it all.

It began with Zeus who, although he was the top Greek god and as such should have been setting a good example, was actually a bit of a philanderer. Among his many amorous adventures, he fell in love with one of his wife's priestesses, a beautiful young lady called Io. Unfortunately, Mrs. Zeus (Hera) found out about these goings on and was out for Io's blood, so in order to protect the girl from his wife's wrath, Zeus changed her into a beautiful white cow and, to compensate her a little for loss of enjoyment of human life, provided her with a field of tasty flowers to graze upon. The Greek word for Io's flower was *ion*. When this became a Latin word, however, the Romans changed it a bit to make it conform to how they thought that a word should be and it ended up as *viola*.

Hera was not content to let Io just wander around eating nice flowers, so she sent a cloud of stinging flies to drive Io out of the field, and out of Greece, for that matter. Poor Io roamed around all over that part of the world now called Ionia after her and eventually swam across from Europe to Asia by way of the Bosporus (Latin *bos* means cow and *porus* means passage) and in time ended up in Egypt, where she gave birth to one of Zeus' many illegitimate sons. Finally, Zeus sent her up into the heavens, beyond the ionosphere, to become a star, well a moon actually, one of Jupiter's, which is fairly appropriate since Jupiter and Zeus are one and the same, depending on whether you're Roman or Greek.

20

So, after all that, it's hardly surprising that we have a violet which is as fair as the star which Io has become.

Apart from looking pretty and smelling nice, violets also earned a place in herbal medicine. Western doctors, finding antiseptic and expectorant qualities in the leaves and flowers, used them to treat coughs and bronchitis, while the Chinese made poultices from them to heal wounds. But since Zeus had made them tasty as a treat for his beloved cow, people began to eat them too, as a flavoring for cakes and pastries, made into a syrup with sugar known as 'Iosaccar' and as the candied flowers themselves. Perfumiers ex-tracted the essential oils and used it to produce expensive perfumes. Even the girl's name was used scientifically in the giving of names to new discoveries which had some semblance of the color of violets, which is how the ionosphere mentioned above got its name. Nowadays, the way oils and juices are extracted results in a different hue, iodine.

Napoleon Bonaparte gave a bunch of violets to his empress Josephine on every wedding anniversary, and when he died, a locket around his neck was found to hold a lock of her hair and a dried violet flower.

There are still a few of us older fellows around who remember buying a bunch of violets from a flower girl in Piccadilly Circus in London for our girl friend, and some of our wives remember the first posy which they were given, even if it wasn't by us.

JUNIPER

Don't tell my mother I'm living in sin,
Don't let the old folks know.
Don't tell my twin that I breakfast on gin,
He'd never survive the blow.

A. P. Herbert, Don't Tell my Mother

A few months ago, a real estate advertisement in our local newspaper made particular mention of a tree, a Rocky Mountain juniper, *Juniperus scopulorum,* which grows on the property which was being advertised. That tree fully deserved to be included as being a feature of the property, because it is rather unusual. Normally this variety of juniper grows east of the Coast Mountains, especially in the Okanagan and from there up into the Rockies, which is why it's called what it is. But it also appears on the islands of the Georgia Basin, although generally in the form of a low shrub. It can often be found along the edges of dry cliffs, near Garry oak and arbutus or madrona trees. However the tree in the advertisement is a beautiful old towering specimen that leaves no doubt that the juniper can also be a magnificent, full-sized tree. In confirmation of that, another common name for this same plant is the Rocky Mountain red cedar and a very close relative, the Virginia juniper, is the tree which is most commonly known as the red cedar throughout much of the United States, except of course here in the Northwest, where we know what a red cedar really is!

Most cedar chests are actually juniper chests and that should give some idea of the scent of the wood of the juniper, which comes from the highly aromatic oils found throughout the entire plant, including the little hard, blue berries which the female plant produces and which take two years to ripen.

In the early French language, the Latin name for this tree, *juniperus,* eventually evolved into *geneve.* The city of Geneva gets its name from the forests of juniper which grew there. The Dutch took the word *geneve* and turned it into 'jenever.' They then got the very smart idea of using the aromatic berries to add flavor to clear alcohol and called the result by the same name as the plants. In 1689, a Dutchman, William of Orange, became King of England and took some of his native habits across there with him, including jenever drinking. It did not take long for his new subjects to follow his example and the name was again altered and shortened into gin. The recipe was also altered slightly and the English variety became known as London gin, while the original Dutch form was called Hollands gin or Geneva gin.

At first, by keeping the price very low, at about a penny a glass, gin drinking was officially encouraged in England, for the sale of the grain needed to distil the alcohol made excellent profits for the ruling landed gentry. But the widespread alcoholism which resulted from this led to terrible social consequences, particularly among the poor, and eventually it also led to an increased death rate. This created a serious shortage of labor and the inevitable demand for higher wages from those still around to work. Since the number of employers being forced to pay these higher wages far outnumbered the landed gentry profiting from selling grain, parliament was finally forced to do something about it. In 1751, parliament placed a high tax on liquor sales. Nearly two hundred and fifty years later, we're still paying it.

All this talk of gin isn't meant to send a reader to the liquor cabinet to fetch a dry martini. Gin has its place in the world of flowers too. Paperwhite Narcissi, which many of us grow in pots to bloom around Christmas time, tend to get tall and leggy and to fall over unless they are staked and tied. But if their pots are watered regularly with a mixture of one tablespoon of gin to a cup of lukewarm water, the plants will stay sturdy, the leaves and stems will remain upright and there will be no need for untidy-looking stakes and string. Vodka doesn't work, nor does rum or whiskey, so it has to be something in the juniper oils which have this effect. And even though the paperwhite bulbs probably come from Holland, they don't need Hollands gin. London gin works fine and, despite the taxes, it's cheaper.

VETCH

But while men slept, his enemy came and sowed tares amongst his wheat.

The Gospel according to St. Matthew

And according to the Oxford English Dictionary, a 'tare' is common vetch, *Vicia sativa*, which is a member of the pea family and which grows wild all over our area. It also grows in Israel, for it appears in my book of wildflowers of the Negev under its botanic name, even though the rest of the book is written in Hebrew and I can't understand it.

There is nothing intrinsically wrong with common vetch. It is not poisonous and, in fact, it is often used as an animal fodder in Europe, mixed with oats. So why was it such a dirty trick to sow them in somebody's wheat field?

Like most of the pea family, vetch is a trailing vine which weaves its way among the stems of grasses and grains and is virtually impossible to separate from them. The farmer in the Bible must have had plenty of cheap labor available to him, for that was how he decided to tackle the problem. "In the time of harvest I will say to the reapers, Gather ye together first the tares and bind them in bunches to burn them."

Despite the labor involved, it was about the only choice which he had, for had he left the vetch where it was and harvested it along with the wheat, he could never have separated the little pealike vetch seeds from the grains of wheat after they were threshed and eventually he would have had to grind them together to make his flour. The effect of the vetch flour mixed in with the wheat flour is that the mixture will not rise, regardless of what is done to leaven it and this would make the mixture totally useless for baking bread and destroy its entire value as a crop. If one tried to make bread dough, all one

24

would end up with would be a sort of thick pea soup.

So one way or another, either in labor costs or crop loss, the sowing of tares among the wheat was not a nice thing to do. To save the wheat, the tares had to be gathered separately and destroyed. That, of course, was the point of the story.

Apart from the common vetch, there are several other varieties of this species growing here. The most striking on these is the cow vetch, *Vicia cracca*, a perennial plant whose bright rosy purple flowers are tightly packed together, looking like a colorful bottle brush at the end of the stems. The vines grow to about four feet or so in length, binding themselves to whatever they touch with long tendrils. This characteristic was responsible for the botanic name, which comes from the same word, *vincere*, to overpower, as we saw in the periwinkle.

As to where that farmer's enemy got his nasty idea, it may be worth noting that among the various unpleasant activities which God ordered the prophet Ezekiel to perform was to take "wheat and barley and beans and lentils and millet and fitches (vetches)," make bread from this and eat the mess for three hundred and ninety days. During this time Ezekiel had to lie on one side only and bake his bread with cow dung.

The farmer's enemy wasn't so unkind after all, was he?

DOGWOOD

Then a very great war-man called Billy the Norman,
Cried Damn it, I never liked my land;
It would be much more handy to leave this Normandy
And live in yon beautiful island.
Thomas Dibdin, The Snug Little Island

What have dogs got to do with dogwoods? Absolutely nothing!

One fine spring morning in the year 1026, Arlette, the beautiful young daughter of a French tanner, went down to the stream outside their cottage to wash her clothes. As she knelt in the sunshine, scrubbing away, Robert Duke of Normandy came riding along and was so struck by the girl's beauty that he instantly asked her to come and live with him at his castle at Falaise. Although Robert was already married, Arlette went with him, bore him a son the following year, whom they named William, and lived with him until his death seven years later.

William was an only child and as he grew up, he became determined that he should inherit his father's lands and titles. However, the local nobility despised 'William the Bastard' as they called him and tried to persuade France's king that the inheritance should not go to Robert's illegitimate offspring. But William retaliated against them with such ferocity that King Henry gave in to him, if only to put an end to all the bloodshed, and confirmed his title to be William, Duke of Normandy.

Robert had a sister, who in her own way was just as ambitious as her nephew. As a young woman, she had crossed the English Channel, married King Ethelred, had by him a son named Edward and, when Ethelred died, had gone on to marry his successor, King Canute.

After Canute's death, Edward came to the throne, a pious and God-fearing man who spent so much of his time on his knees, confessing his sins, that he has come down to us in history as Edward the Confessor. He married but had no children and, back in Normandy, Duke William saw his chance. A quick visit to Auntie Emma, a chat with Cousin Edward and William returned home to Falaise, certain that Edward would name him as his successor to the throne of England.

But things didn't work out that way. As Edward lay dying, his wife convinced him to name her brother Harold as the future king and, on

January 5, 1066, on Edward's death, Harold claimed the crown.

William was not the only one to be angered by this. In exile in Norway, Harold's half brother Tostig was seen by the Norse king as a much better prospect for Viking control of England than was Harold. Accordingly he equipped an invasion force to depose Harold and replace him with Tostig, who had sworn to be his vassal.

Meanwhile William was not letting the grass grow under his feet. He, too, raised a huge army to invade England and place him on the throne, which had been promised to him.

Tostig landed first, advanced to York but was met and beaten by Harold's English army at the battle of Stamford Bridge. But before Harold and his soldiers could even get their breath back, word came that William had landed in force at Pevensey Bay on the south coast. Harold collected his weary troops and marched them 200 miles south to London in seven days, where he raised reinforcements, then on again to take up position on the evening of October 13, 1066, on a hillside outside the town of Hastings, only eight miles from Pevensey Bay, blocking the invaders' route to London.

The next morning, the well-rested Norman army attacked. All day the battle raged, the Norman cavalry and archers pouring everything they had against the densely packed English lines, which would not break. As evening approached, William changed his tactics and ordered a sham retreat. Most of the jubilant English broke ranks and rushed downhill after the enemy, leaving Harold surrounded only by his personal bodyguard. But a small group of Norman archers had remained in hiding while their comrades pretended to flee. A volley of arrows was shot high into the air and one of the shafts struck Harold in the eye, inflicting a mortal wound. And William the Bastard became William the Conqueror for the rest of time.

What has all of this got to do with dogwoods? We're getting to that.

William was not a rich man. He did not have the money to equip, transport and pay a large army, so he had come up with the original scheme of making the invasion of England a business enterprise in which he sold shares to other French nobles in return for their supplying men, horses and ships. If he won the English crown these shares would pay a dividend in the form of captured English estates. So, after the battle, many of these old manors became occupied by new French masters and their families, whom they had brought to England to avoid the costs of maintaining homes in both countries. The common laborers on these estates remained from the previous English owners and had to adapt themselves as best they could to their new overlords.

In those days, before the advent of modern methods of cookery, meat was often cooked like kebabs are today, in small pieces, skewered and roasted over an open fire. The skewers were called 'prickes' for the simple reason that they were pricked through the meat. Since skewers should be made from a strong wood, which neither imparts a flavor to the meat, nor leaves splinters, one particular shrub had been found by experience to produce the best timber for the job. The wood had come to be known as 'pricke timber' and the shrub as the 'pricke timber tree.'

The new Norman landowners didn't speak English and had no intention of learning the language. They had brought with them as part of their military armaments a narrow, pointed, steel weapon which they called a *dague*. Their English servants had to use this word when they talked to their masters, but pronounced it as 'dagge,' which soon became the word which stays with us today, a 'dagger.' In the kitchens of the manor houses, where pig became *porc*, sheep became *mouton* and oxen was *boeuf*, a pricke began to be called a dagge too, because of its similarity to the weapon's blade, coupled with a rather limited vocabulary of French words on the part of the kitchen staff. In turn, the pricke timber tree became the dagge timber tree, then, as timber gave way to

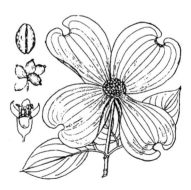

wood in common terminology, the dagge wood tree. Within a couple of centuries people called it the dogge wood tree and eventually it ended up as we know it today, the dogwood tree and Dagwood remains only as the name of Mr. Bumstead of cartoon fame.

I suppose that it wouldn't have sounded quite right to have had the pricke timber tree flower as the provincial emblem of B.C. So, for what it's worth, thank you Arlette.

28

BROOM

O, the broom, the bonnie, bonnie broom,
The broom o' the Cowden knowes;
Fain would I be in my ain country,
Herdin' my faither's yowes.

Traditional Scots song

And there are plenty of people around here who wish that the broom had stayed on the Cowden hills; and who, if they knew it, would curse the name of Captain Walter Colquhoun Grant, the gallant former officer of The Royal Scots Greys, who first introduced this plant to Vancouver Island in 1849. In less than 150 years, the three broom plants which he managed to germinate from seed have multiplied a millionfold and spread throughout the entire Pacific Northwest, in much the same way as the spread of European starlings across the whole continent since sixty of them were released in New York's Central Park in 1890.

On the other hand, many people like to see the bright yellow flowers of the Scotch broom, which are most abundant in April and May, but which can appear in smaller numbers almost any month of the year.

John Gerard's description of the plant, written in 1597, is as good as any. "Broome is a bush or shrubby plant. It hath stalks or rather woody branches, from which do spring slender twigs, cornered, green, tough...many times divided into small branches about which do grow little leaves of an obscure green colour and brave yellow floures."

The common name for the plant arose from the use of the "many times divided" branches and twigs, tied together into bundles, as brooms to sweep the floor. The second word in the botanic name, *Cytisus scoparius*, is the Latin word for such a broom. The first word is said to relate to the Greek island of Cythera, where the species was thought to have originated.

As well as the usual yellow-flowered variety, there is a variety with rusty red colors mixed with the yellow, and a Spanish broom, which flowers later in the season and has slightly paler yellow blooms and a less noticeable scent. Both are fairly common in this area.

Our local black-tailed deer seem to be particularly fond of broom

29

Broome

flowers and we see them frequently in the spring, teaching their fawns that this is good food.

The seeds of the broom bush grow in about two-inch long pods like little peas and when they dry in the hot summer sun, the pods suddenly split open with an audible crack, flinging the seeds away to the ground, sometimes several feet from the plant. An oil in the seeds is attractive to ants, which carry them off to their underground nests. Birds too enjoy them, but some of the seeds are so hard that they just pass through and fall onto the ground, wrapped in natural fertilizer and it is such characteristics as these that have brought about the extremely rapid spread of this plant in this areas.

The old Latin name for broom was *genista*. When the name passed into French, it became *genet* and the *planta genet* became the emblem of the French Dukes of Anjou. On December 19, 1154, Henry of Anjou, great-grandson of William the Conqueror, was crowned King of England, starting the 300-year reign of the Plantagenet family, which ended at the Battle of Bosworth Field on August 22, 1485. Richard III, the last of the Plantagenets and the last King of England to die in battle, did so wearing not the broom badge of his Anjou ancestors, but the white rose of York. Unseated from his charger, he fought on foot until he was finally struck down crying, so Shakespeare tells us, "My kingdom for a horse."

30

SORREL

He, not unlike the great ones of mankind,
Disfigures earth; and, plotting in the dark,
Toils much to earn a monumental pile,
That may record the mischiefs he has done.

William Cowper, The Task

We can all think of people who fit that description.

In the officers' messes of Scottish army regiments, all water is removed from the dining table after dinner, before the toast to the queen is proposed. This tradition dates back to the founding of those regiments after the Jacobite rebellion of 1745. At that time, many Scots believed that Charles Edward Stuart, Bonnie Prince Charlie, was the true King of England and Scotland, and not the German King George who was on the throne. But following the failure of the rebellion, when English Catholics chose not to join in the attempt to overthrow the Protestant ruler, the Highland army was defeated at the Battle of Cullodden and Charles fled into exile in France, across the North Sea or as they said in Scotland, "Over the water."

It was obviously disloyal to King George, possibly even treasonous, for his officers to drink a toast to his rival, so the crafty Scots raised their glasses to "The King," but then passed them over tumblers of water on the table to signify that they were toasting not King George, but the king over the water, Bonnie Prince Charlie. When the commanders of the British army in London found out about this, they ordered that all water should be removed from the table before the loyal toast was drunk. And it still happens that way today.

The Irish, too, had a disloyal toast of their own aimed at King William III, otherwise known as King Billy, who had beaten the Irish forces at the Battle of the Boyne in 1690. Twelve years later, to quote Sir Winston Churchill, "On February 20, 1702, William was riding in the park round Hampton Court on Sorrel, a favourite horse. Sorrel stumbled in the new workings of a mole and the king was thrown." William died a few days later and the Irish, who until then had been toasting the devil, whom they hoped would come and take King Billy, changed their toast to Sorrel, who had done the job quite satisfactorily on his behalf.

31

Sorrel has long been a fairly common name for a horse of a particular color—a sorrel-color, or in other words, the reddish brown hue of the seed head of the common sorrel plant, *Rumex acetosa*. This is one of the most prolific of all wildflowers, spreading by both seeds and by thin underground runners, so that it has invaded almost every field, garden and road side. Its common name comes from the Old German word *sur*, which has become 'sour' in English. In France, the plant was called *surelle* and its leaves were often used in salads. After the Battle of Hastings and the

imposition of French on the kitchen staffs of the manor houses, *surelle* passed into English and evolved into the sorrel which we have today.

The *Rumex* family name goes back a long way, to at least as far as the Roman naturalist Pliny, in the first century A.D. He used it for what we now call 'dock,' which belongs to the same family as Sorrel. We have dock growing here, which is known botanically as *Rumex occidentalis* or western dock. *Acetosa* means acidic and is an apt description of the sour-lemon taste of the sorrel leaves, which are still cultivated both commercially and in home gardens for use in cooking.

In Elizabethan times, the juice squeezed from sorrel leaves was mixed with crabapple juice and unripe grapes to produce a condiment called verjuice, which was used in place of vinegar. What it must have tasted like can be imagined, perhaps, from a remark made by Thomas Heywood, a dramatist and contemporary of Shakespeare, when he wrote, "She scarce will let me kisse her but she makes vergisse faces."

Maybe he should have used Certs.

And in case you're wondering about the significance of that quotation up above, Cowper was not talking about a person, his poem was referring to a mole.

DANDELIONS

What's in a name? That which we call a Rose
By any other name would smell as sweet.
William Shakespeare, Romeo and Juliet

Piss-a-beds grow beside the road outside our house. So do Irish daisies and priest's crowns, blowballs and devil's milk pails along with heart fever grass and dandelions.

"At last," you might think, "There's something I know—a dandelion." But in fact all of these are names for the same plant and there are plenty more names than these for this common little yellow flower.

The problem with common names is that they sometimes tend to be fairly local and what a flower is called in one village might well differ from the name by which it is known, two miles down the road. Conversely, one single common name might be applied to a host of different plants from place to place so that, for example, the black-eyed Susan of one county might not even belong to the same family as the black-eyed Susan of somewhere else. All of this creates problems when one is talking about wildflowers to someone who has not been brought up in the same locality as oneself.

Back in 1753, Carl von Linné, a Swedish botanist, published a book called *Species Plantarum* (the species of plants) in which he used for the first time a system of classification which he had been devising for twenty years and which was the foundation of modern plant nomenclature. Actually, it is used to classify every living thing, including Carl himself, who has come to be known under his binomial or two-name system as Carolus Linnaeus. It is a very simple idea at heart.

DANDELION.
LEONTODON TARAXACUM.

Everything belongs to some species or another, let's say the Jones species. Then there are varieties of Jones, for example, Peters and Annes. So if someone is called a Jones, Anne, one knows who is being talked about and that it's neither a Jones, Peter nor a Smith, William. The language which he chose to use for his system was Latin, which was the closest thing there was to a universal language in those days. But he had to Latinize words and names from other languages, particularly from Greek, to achieve his end results. Where possible he used the old Roman name, which, of course, was already in Latin, but where that was not possible, because many of the world's plants had never even been seen by the Romans, he devised names based on characteristics of the plant itself or, in some cases, the name of the person who first identified the plant as a new species. That's how we have plant species named *Lewisias* and *Clarkias*, after the same Captains Lewis and Clark who appeared in the Camas essay.

And so the piss-a-bed and the dandelion became the *Taraxacum officinale*, partly from a combination of two Greek words, *taraxos* and *akos*, meaning a remedy for a disorder and the rest being the latin word *officinale*, which signifies in herbal medicine that the plant is officially recognized as having effective curative properties. The disorder which this plant could cure was urine retention, for it works as a diuretic, its effectiveness being reflected in the piss-a-bed name.

A lot of people are scared of botanic names and have convinced themselves that they are too difficult to learn because they're in a foreign language. Yet these same people have had no problem in learning other foreign names, Mao Tse Tung, Mikhail Gorbachov, Indira Ghandi, Luciano Pavarotti and even Wayne Gretzky. In fact, most of us are more at home talking about a Monica Seles than we would be if we were trying to pronounce those good old British names, Cholmondley and Dalziel, which should properly sound like Chumley and De-el.

Remembering a botanic name is easier if one knows what it means or where it comes from. It also makes the plant itself a bit more interesting and that's the whole aim of this book.

As for the word dandelion, it comes from the French *dent de lion* meaning a lion's tooth, for the edges of the leaves of this plant are deeply indented into long toothlike shapes, which obviously reminded some Frenchman in the dim and distant past of lions.

34

FOXGLOVES

Foxglove and Nightshade, side by side,
Emblems of Punishment and Pride.

Sir Walter Scott, Lady of the Lake

Very few people today know the name of Leonhart Fuchs, a sixteenth-century German physician and botanist, although he is commemorated by a plant known to almost every gardener, the fuchsia. The reason he's mentioned here is that he was responsible for giving what became the botanic name to one of our more common local wildflowers, the foxglove.

The German common name for this plant is *fingerhut*, meaning a thimble, which is a fair enough description of each of the little flowers. The Latin for something which pertains to a finger is *digitalis* or "of the digit" and this is the name which Fuchs gave to the plant and the one which is still in use worldwide, more than 400 years later.

The English were, perhaps, more imaginative in the common names which they used for this plant, which ranged from fairies' petticoats to foxes' gloves. The second of these is the older of the two, because the word petticoat did not enter the English language until after the Norman invasion in 1066, but about 100 years before that, an Anglo-Saxon named Bald, who was a friend of King Alfred (the one who burned the cakes while he was hiding out in a cow herd's hut and was so busy cleaning his weapons that he didn't notice that the housewife's cakes, which he was meant to be watching, were overcooking on the griddle), paid a ghost writer scribe named Cild to write a book about medical treatments. This ended up being entitled *The Leech Book of Bald* and in it, the plant which we're talking about was referred to as a "foxes glofa."

The ancient Greeks knew the foxglove as Appollonaris, their legends saying that it had been a gift from the god, Appollo, to his son, Aesculapius, the god of medicine. But despite this connection with medicine, there is no evidence that the plant was used by either the Greeks or the Romans and even as late as 1597, John Gerard, the herbalist, was writing, "They are of no use, neither have they any place amongst medicines, according to the ancients."

It was not until about 200 years later that Dr. William Withering, who was carrying out an investigation of herbal cures, came across the use of foxglove tea by certain ladies in Shropshire as a remedy for dropsy, a condition which may be a symptom of heart disease. Dr. Withering confirmed the effectiveness of the foxglove for this purpose and from then on, digitalis joined the growing list of officially recognized medicinal plants. Today, its chemical constituents are still used to assist patients suffering from congestive heart failure.

Our local wild foxglove is the *Digitalis purpurea*, the second word meaning that the flower is colored purple. Pink and white flowers are almost as common and most of the flowers have little leopard spots inside the petal. It is a tall plant, anywhere from three to six feet in height, rising from a rosette of large, downy leaves. The flowers cluster

Purple Fox-gloves

up the single stem, generally on the side which receives the most light. Foxgloves are often seen near road sides, where whatever moisture is available has ended up in the ditches and the clearing of trees for the road allowance provides for a period of sunshine to fall on the growing plants. The foxglove is biennial, that is to say that the seed germinates and grows part way one year, but the flowers do not appear until the second year of its life.

Anyone tempted to experiment with this very dangerous plant should remember the words of another herbalist, Nicholas Culpepper. "It is best not to meddle with it, lest the cure should end in the churchyard."

WORMWOOD

The most magnificent and costly dome
Is but the upper chamber to a tomb.
Rev. Edward Young, The Last Day

In 353 B.C. the fairly insignificant governor of the Persian province of
Caria died peacefully in his bed. He had not made much of a mark
during his lifetime, but because he was fully aware of this, he decided
that the only way that he would be remembered by future generations
was to be buried in the most magnificent tomb in the world. So he set
about designing it for himself.

After his death, his widow, who happened also to be his sister and his
successor as governor—they liked to keep things in the family—had the
tomb built exactly as he had planned it and the huge white marble
edifice quickly became one of the Seven Wonders of the Ancient World,
joining such famous company as King Nebuchadnezzar's Hanging
Gardens in Babylon, the Sphinx and the Pyramids.

This vast sepulchre, pieces of which can still be seen in the British
Museum in London, was the first building ever to be called a mauso-
leum, for the simple reason that the corpse which it housed was that of
the late governor Mausolus. And the name of the woman responsible
for having this great wonder built was Artemesia.

The world often remembers people only by their tombs. If it wasn't for
the Great Pyramid, who would ever have heard of Cheops? Mumtaz
Mahal has only come down to us in history because she was the
favourite wife of a Mogul emperor, who could afford to build the Taj
Mahal over her grave. And then there's Tutenkhamen, of course,
although he is remembered more for what was in his tomb than for the
tomb itself. But who remembers those loyal and loving survivors who
arranged for these memorials to be built?

Well, at least as far as Artemesia is concerned, botanists and gardeners
do, for her name has come down through history as that of a family of
plants which, around here, includes the *Artemesia tridentata*, the common sagebrush of the dry interior; the *Artemesia dracunculus*, which
only grows in herb gardens and goes by the common name of tarragon;
and the *Artemesia suksdorfii*, usually known as wormwood. The second

part of the botanic name commemorates Wilhelm Suksdorf, a local plant collector who died only sixty years ago.

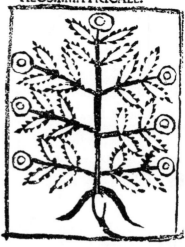

HERBA ARTEMISIA LEPTA. FILOS.I.MATRICALE.

Wormwood contains a bitter oil which, when it was extracted from the European variety of this plant, was thought to be able to drive worms from the body, in much the same way as deworming pills for dogs act today. This is where the name wormwood originated. The scent of the plant, either fresh or dried, has been known for centuries to keep away moths and fleas, so bunches of it were often hung inside houses. Nicholas Culpepper, a famous seventeenth-century English herbalist, recommended it as a cure for "the hypochondriacal disorders of sedentary men," whatever they might be. But the German name for the plant, *wermuth*, gives the clue to the most popular use of the herb today, as a flavoring for vermouth.

In fact, wormwood and alcohol go back a long way together. In the Old Testament book, The Lamentations of Jeremiah, we find, "He hath made me drunk with wormwood." Jeremiah would have had good cause to lament the aftermath of a drunken binge with wormwood flavored liquor, particularly if it was anything like the version which was made in France until about eighty years ago, which also had some anise added to it and went by the name absinthe. It was while he was under the influence of this beverage that the Dutch painter, Van Gogh, cut off his own ear, which probably made him lament a bit, too, the next morning.

So because of wormwood and tarragon and their cousins, Artemesia's name is remembered after nearly 2250 years. And if you hadn't heard of him before you read this, you may well remember Governor Mausolus too.

ARBUTUS OR MADRONE

Oh Captain, my Captain! Our fearful trip is done,
The ship has weathered every rack,
The prize we sought is won.

Walt Whitman, Oh Captain, my Captain

It must have been a source of considerable annoyance to those stern disciplinarians, the captains of Royal Navy ships in the eighteenth and nineteenth centuries, to have to put up with all of the mess of nursery gardens on the neat and clean decks of their vessels. But orders are orders and their superiors had decreed that many of them should carry naturalists on board. For Princess Augusta, the mother of King George III had created a botanic garden at her palace at Kew, outside London and she needed new and exotic plants for it. So too did John Churchill, Duke of Marlborough, the country's great military hero, for his new estate at Blenheim. His new digs were being built for him as a gift from the grateful taxpayers and being landscaped by the famous landscape architect, 'Capability' Brown. And with no disrespect to those who gave the captains their orders, their Lordships of the Admiralty, those were also the days when a nice profit could often be made from the sale of new plants which the naturalists brought back with them.

So the captains had to grin and bear it while their ships' decks sprouted trees and shrubs from earth-filled boxes. Cold frames filled with foreign flowers covered the quarter decks and dirty little men with watering cans ran around, getting in the way of proper sailors. For these ships were at sea for up to three years at a time and the carefully collected plants could not just be packed away in a hold, but had to be grown on in full daylight, in soil in containers, until they returned to England. And very sophisticated some of these containers became, because tropical plants had to be brought round the tip of South America, close to the Antarctic ice pack, and they could not be allowed to freeze.

All of the famous British maritime explorers of that era carried naturalists along with them. Captain James Cook, circumnavigating the world on the *Endeavour*, had Joseph Banks, who went on to become the director of the botanic gardens at Kew. Vice-admiral Robert Fitzroy of the *Beagle* carried Charles Darwin and we all know what he did later. Sir John Franklin, on two of his expeditions to the Canadian Arctic, trying to find a northwest passage to the Pacific, was accompanied by John Richardson, who was knighted, eventually, for his work as a map maker as well as for his naturalist activities. And in my own part of the world, Puget Sound and Georgia Strait, Captain George Vancouver had Archibald Menzies for company on the *Discovery*.

Like Darwin and Richardson, Menzies studied medicine at Edinburgh University but unlike them, he had to work his way through college and did so by laboring as an assistant gardener at the Edinburgh Botanic Gardens. Medicine and botany were, of course, still closely allied in those days.

All four of these naturalists had plants named after them. *Banksias* are a species of evergreen trees and shrubs which Banks discovered in Australia. The Chilean barberry is called the *Berberis darwinii*. *Artemesia richardsonii* is a dwarf relative of wormwood which grows on the shores of Banks Island in the Canadian Arctic, named after the same Joseph Banks by Richardson, as part of his map making duties. And here in the Georgia Basin and along the Pacific Coast we have that most beautiful of all of our native trees and the largest member of the Heather family, the *Arbutus menziesii*, along with a little blue larkspur, the *Delphinium menziesii* and the false azalea, *Menziesia ferruginea*.

But Spanish explorers sailing up from Mexico also named plants which they found and they, too, had seen the beautiful arbutus. For the mother of Jesus, they called it Madrona and that remains its common name in the United States.

As a footnote, Banks, Menzies and the others were followers of a long tradition. When another English explorer, Martin Frobisher, reached the coast of Labrador in 1576, he sent some of his crew ashore to search the land and bring back to the ship "whatsoever thing they could find...in token of Christian possession." Some brought back flowers.

WILD ONIONS

Let onion atoms lurk within the bowl,
And, scarce suspected, animate the whole.

Rev. Sidney Smith, Recipe for salad.

On 15 December, 1790, the sailing vessel *Discovery* was commissioned at London and placed under the command of Commander George Vancouver, Royal Navy. Armed with ten fourpounders guns and ten swivel guns and with a crew of 134 all told, the ship set sail in March 1791, under orders to proceed to the northwest coast of America for the purpose of acquiring a more complete knowledge of it.

When Archibald Menzies came on board to perform his duties as ship's surgeon and naturalist, Vancouver noted the arrival in his journal and added rather pompously that "Mr. Menzies has doubtless given sufficient proof of his abilities to qualify him for the station which it is intended he should fill."

On June 8th, 1792, a small party of sailors from the *Discovery*, including Menzies, climbed ashore on Orcas Island in the San Juans, in order to acquire knowledge. And, if nothing else, Menzies showed that his years of work as an assistant gardener had not been wasted and that his abilities included that of being able to tell an onion when he met one.

"I found here a small, well-tasted wild onion," he wrote in his diary that night, when he got back on board ship, "which grew in little tufts in the crevices of the rocks."

Although Menzies did not identify it in more detail than that, it was probably the Hooker's onion, *Allium acuminatum*, which was named in honor of Sir William Hooker, the first director of the Royal Botanic Gardens at Kew. *Allium* is just the old Roman name for an onion and *acuminatum* means narrow pointed, for the petals of this particular onion are shaped that way. Up to twenty-five of these bright magenta colored flowers cluster together at the top of a six to eight-inch high stem. The grasslike leaves shrivel and die before the flower appears, leaving only it and its stem to mark where the bulb lies beneath the ground.

Other wild onions grow around here. The first of these is the nodding

onion, *Allium cernuum*. The second of these words refers to a shepherd's crook, and, as this name implies, the top of the stem of this variety bends over near the top, so that the loose bunch of small pink flowers hangs down, like an umbrella suspended from its point.

Another local onion, especially prevalent at the higher elevations of the mountains surrounding the Georgia Basin, is the Geyer's onion, *Allium geyerii*, named after Carl Geyer, a botanist who identified this variety in Washington State in 1844. It too has small pink flowers, but they point upwards and, after they die, they leave at the top of the stalk a small round ball of tiny onion bulbs, called bulbils, which form the next year's seeds.

After the *Discovery* returned to London, Menzies was sent off once more, this time to the West Indies and, when that trip ended, he resigned from the navy and set up practice as a doctor in London. He was later elected President of the Linnean Society, Britain's oldest biology society, which is still active and which owns Linnaeus' original plant collection.

LOTUS

Dark faces, pale against the rosy flame,
The mild-eyed, melancholy Lotos eaters came.
Branches they bore of that enchanted stem,
Laden with flower and fruit....

Alfred, Lord Tennyson, The Lotus Eaters

Those of us who inhabit this favored little corner of the world are often accused of "living in Lotusland." Homer is to blame for that. He got the idea of a "Land of the Lotus Eaters" when he was writing the *Odyssey* around 2,500 years or so ago and he gave to the lotus the power of producing in those who ate it a state of dreamy forgetfulness and the loss of any desire whatever to return home. Ulysses' ship's crew got into the lotus bowl at one stage and he had a heck of a job getting them all back on board and on their way home again.

Doctor Samuel Johnson, who wrote the first ever *Dictionary of the English Language*, appears to have suffered the same fate on the Isle of Skye, off the west coast of Scotland. Although he did not think much of Scotland itself when he visited it ("Seeing Scotland, Madame, is only seeing a worse England"), the western isles were a different matter altogether and he wrote of Dunvegan, the main village on Skye and the ancestral home of Clan McLeod, "At Dunvegan I have tasted Lotus and was in danger of forgetting that I was ever to depart."

It was probably the local single malt whisky which he tasted, as it is known to have a remarkably similar effect.

There's obviously no point in trying for a surprise at this stage, with a "guess what...lotus grows here too" routine. But yes, we do have wild lotus growing in this area, two different ones in fact. These are the *Lotus micranthus*, or small-flowered lotus, and the *Lotus corniculatis*, commonly called the bird's foot trefoil.

This second common name is one of those marvels of plant nomenclature

43

where whoever assigned that name got it all wrong. Trefoil means three-leaved, like clover. The leaves of this lotus grow in groups of five. As for the bird's foot part, virtually every bird has four toes, apart from the three-toed woodpecker, and certainly not five. However the plant does look quite like a little yellow clover, so perhaps that's where the confusion arose.

The small-flowered lotus is not quite as common, but it is by no means rare and, like its cousin, generally grows in dry, grassy areas in full sunshine. Its tiny pale yellow flower, tinged with pink, is extremely beautiful if one takes the trouble to look at it closely.

And for those who thought that a lotus was some sort of a water lily, that's right too, for there is a tropical water lily, native to Egypt but now found in many tropical countries, whose botanic name is *Nymphaea lotus*, which has become a symbol of Buddha.

So which of these did the lotus-eaters eat? None of them. Most experts have identified Homer's lotus as being a shrub which grows in North Africa, the jujube tree or *Zizyphus lotus*, which produces a small, sweet-tasting berry. For many years now, this berry has been copied as a little gelatinous candy, artificially colored and sweetened and sold as a jujube.

HAWTHORN

The hawthorn bush, with seats beneath the shade,
For talking age and whispering lovers made.
Oliver Goldsmith, The Deserted Village

Somewhere around the year 1130, William of Malmesbury wrote a history of an ancient church at Glastonbury in England. Glastonbury is best known for its connections with the legend of King Arthur and many people believe it to be Avalon, where the stories say that he was buried. In fact, about sixty years after William wrote his history, excavations at the old church revealed, at a depth of seven feet, a large stone slab, beneath which was a coffin hollowed from an oak tree, containing the skeletons of a man and a woman. On top of the slab lay a lead cross, inscribed in Latin, "Here lies interred in the Island of Avalon the renowned King Arthur."

But Avalon goes back further in legend than the days of King Arthur, for it was on the shore near there that, according to William's books, Saint Joseph of Arimathea is said to have landed, having been sent to Britain shortly after the Crucifiction of Christ, to spread the word to the pagans.

After walking inland from the beach for a while, St. Joseph became tired and rested for a few hours on what is now called Wearyall Hill. Before he lay down, he stuck his staff of hawthorn wood into the ground. While he slept, it took root and so he left it there when he went on his way. From then on it flourished and blossomed each year on Christmas Day. A hawthorn bush, said locally to be directly descended from St. Joseph's staff, still grows on the hill and blooms in early January which, in the old calendar, would have been Christmastide.

Hawthorn also grows all round the Georgia Basin and on the islands, but it is not the same variety as the Glastonbury thorn. That, perhaps in confirmation of the legend, is a *Crataegus oxyacantha*, which is a native of the Middle East. Ours is the black hawthorn, so named

45

because its berries are black, as opposed to the red fruit of most hawthorns. Its botanic name is *Crataegus douglasii*. The first word comes from the Greek for strong, which is an apt description of the wood and it because it is so strong that it is still used for staffs and clubs. The second word commemorates the Scottish botanist, David Douglas, after whom the Douglas fir is also named, who first identified this hawthorn in this area.

In most places, including here, the hawthorn blooms in May, hence its other common name, the May or Mayflower, which the Pilgrim Fathers named their ship after. Our black hawthorn is a tall and bushy shrub, with a height of up to twelve feet. It has a rough bark and sharp thorns of about an inch in length. It was these thorns and the strength of the wood in the stems which made this plant such a favorite as a hedge shrub to stop animals from invading farm fields and the old hedgers would plant brambles and briars and honeysuckle to weave in among the branches and give thickness and body to the planting and cover for the birds which would come to live there. These old Hawthorn hedge rows were highly developed natural systems, their intricate complexities evolving over hundreds of years, supporting self-sustaining communities of birds and insects, small mammals, plants and even the country folk who came to pick berries in autumn and firewood from the dead branches. Hawthorn berries were just one of the sources of medicine found in the hedges and they are still used medicinally as a treatment for high blood pressures.

An old weather proverb says, "Many Haws, Many Sloes, cold toes." So if the berries are thick on the hawthorns, one might be smart to get the fleece-lined boots ready.

46

SELF HEAL

But now, farewell. I am going a long way...
To the island-valley of Avilion;
Where falls not hail, or rain, or any snow,
Nor ever wind blows loudly; but it lies
Deep-meadow'd, happy, fair with orchard-lawns
And bowery hollows, crowned with summer sea,
Where I will heal me of my grievous wound.

Alfred, Lord Tennyson, Morte d'Arthur

According to Tennyson, those were the last words of the renowned King Arthur, before he went off to Avalon or Glastonbury to die.

One has to presume, therefore, that no soldier's wound wort grows at Avalon, otherwise there is little doubt that the king would indeed have managed to heal himself, for another of that plant's common names is self heal.

It is a mildly amusing coincidence that self heal grows in great abundance in the grass all around our local medical center. One has to wonder if there is some message there to those who would take up the doctor's time with minor ailments. In any event, there it is, self heal, heal all, wound wort or any of a whole collection of common names for the *Prunella vulgaris*.

The word *Prunella* is a corruption of brunella which in turn comes from the German word for a particular illness, *die braune*. According to John Gerard, this was an "infirmitie of soldiers in campe," but it was actually what used to be called quinsey, which is an inflammation of the throat.

Self heal grows in profusion throughout this area, beside roads and wherever else it can spread to. It is a small plant, usually three or four inches tall, with paired dark green leaves and hairy, square stems. The flowers grow in thick, short spikes, each individual bloom within the spike being a deep purple in color and looking like a tiny snapdragon flower. It comes into bloom in July and August and prefers to be in lightly shaded places where there is some moisture in the soil.

The Doctrine of Signatures, the theory that one could tell what illness a plant could cure by observing some similarity between a part of the plant and the affected portion of the body, did occasionally work,

47

although in general it was pretty stupid. Self heal was one of its successes. Because of a similarity in shape between a part of the flower and a billhook, the doctors of the day who believed in the doctrine decided that this plant should obviously be used to treat wounds caused by hooks, scythes, sickles and other such sharp tools. In fact, strong infusions of the dried and powdered plant are effective styptics. In other words, they stop bleeding. John Gerard wrote that "there is no better wounde herbe in the world than Self-heale is." From this use, other common names arose, sickle-wort, hook-weed, carpenter's wort and so on.

This same doctrine was interpreted rather differently in Germany. They saw in the tubular shape of the tiny flowers something which they thought resembled the human throat. Hence the use in Germany to treat *die braune*, which has led to the plant's botanic name.

VERONICA

When in April the sweet showers fall
And pierce the drought of March to the root, and all
The veins are bathed in liquor of such power
As brings about the engendering of the flower,
...Then people long to go on pilgrimages.

Chaucer, Prologue to The Canterbury Tales

In St. Peter's Church in Rome is kept a piece of stained cloth, believed by many devout Catholics to be a handkerchief used by a woman in Jerusalem to wipe the sweat from the face of Christ as he carried his heavy cross toward Calvary. The marks on the cloth are said to reveal a true likeness of Christ's face. In a mixture of Latin and Greek, a true likeness is a *vera iconica* and it was from those words that the name was formed, which was to be given to that anonymous woman, Veronica.

By what some might regard to be a considerable stretch of the imagination, the flower of a small plant which grows freely throughout Europe was thought to have markings which resembled those on the cloth. As a result of this, the flower too was given the name Veronica.

We have all heard the expression that wishes someone "God-speed." That came from an earlier expression, "God speed ye well." In the same way that a similar phrase, "God fare ye well" turned into just "farewell," so the valediction "God speed ye well" became merely "speed well" and happened to be the current colloquialism at the time when people longed to go on pilgrimages, particularly to Rome, where they would kneel before the Holy relics, including Veronica's handkerchief.

As these pilgrims set off from home, their friends would hand them Veronica flowers to wear in their hats as good luck charms and wish them "speed well." And so, in the odd way that things happen, the Veronica flower also became known as a speedwell and both names are

49

Veronica flower also became known as a speedwell and both names are still commonly used today.

We have several members of the speedwell family growing locally. They are all fairly easy to recognize, having small, half-inch wide, pale blue or lilac flowers, whose petals change color to yellow as they approach the center of the bloom. The one most often seen is the slender speedwell, *Veronica filiformis*, on which those poor city folk who know no better spend tens of thousands of dollars, trying to eliminate with chemicals from their would-be perfect lawns.

The next most common is the American brooklime, *Veronica americana*, a slightly more upright plant, yet still rather spindly looking, which one finds growing in ditches and alongside streams. The name 'brooklime' is quite interesting. The Old English name for this plant, before anyone had heard of St. Veronica, was 'hleomoce,' which eventually evolved into 'lemoke.' Those flowers which grew near brooks became known as 'brok-lemoke,' then 'broklemke,' 'brooklyme' and finally 'brooklime.' Since the latin word for mud was *limus* the connection between this flower, streams and mud was recognized from an early age.

A third local variety, the marsh speedwell, *Veronica scutellata*, grows as its name implies in boggy places. It has lilac-colored flowers and its leaves are thin, like those of rosemary. In ditches which dry up in summer, when there are no "sweet showers" to pierce the drought, this plant manages to go through each stage of its growth before the dampness disappears and next spring it is back again to repeat the whole process.

STRAWBERRIES

Wife, into thy garden and set me a plot
Of strawberry rootes of the best to be got.
Thomas Tusser, Instructions to Housewifery

I can imagine the answer I would get to a remark like that. But whether
or not one thinks much of his manners, at least he displayed good taste
in fruit, for he then went on to say,

Such, growing abroade amongst thornes in wood,
Well chosen and picked prove excellent good.

The plant which Mr. Tusser was writing about was the wood strawberry,
Fragaria vesca, which is native both to Europe and to North America.
It grows in this area along with two other varieties of strawberries: the
wild strawberry, *Fragaria virginiana*, whose leaves are distinguishable
from the wood strawberry's by having a bluish tinge to them; and a dark
green leaved Chilean strawberry, *Fragaria chiloensis*. The last words of
those two botanic names are self-explanatory and reflect where the
varieties were first discovered. The flowers of all three sorts are virtually
identical, having five white petals and blooming at the same time from
mid-April through into June. One hopes, however, that no one would
dream of digging any of them up from the wood these days and
transplanting them into a garden plot.

It was from crossbreeding between their own local wood strawberry and
the other two varieties, once they had been brought back to Europe by
explorers and travelers, that many of our present varieties of cultivated
strawberries originated.

Strawberries have long held a place in medicine of both the conven-
tional and the odder practices. In regard to the latter, in the Middle
Ages a theory arose that the remedy for all illnesses lay in plants shaped
like the diseased or injured human organ. Naturally, since a strawberry
was roughly heart-shaped and colored blood red, it had to be prescribed
as a treatment for heart problems. In more normal herbal medicine, the
fruit was used as a laxative, the leaves and roots as a treatment for
diarrhea and the great Linnaeus himself claimed that a tea made with
the leaves had cured his gout. Externally, a lotion made from the fruit
is said to help reduce wrinkles of the skin.

The botanic name *Fragaria* comes from the Latin word *fraga*, which means a strawberry, but which is also the root of the verb *fragare*, to smell sweet, from which our present word fragrant is derived. The French word for the plant came from the same origin but evolved into *fraise*. From that came the word *frasier*, meaning a strawberry grower, which became used as a surname and crossed over to England with William the Conqueror to end up as the Fraser family in Scotland. Sir Simon Fraser, who was led off to his execution with the garland of periwinkle was, in his time, the head of that family, another famous member being his namesake who traveled the Fraser River and after whom Vancouver, B.C.'s Simon Fraser University was named. And if there is a painting of the arms of Clan Fraser at the Fraser Arms Hotel in Vancouver, it should show the armorial shield of Lord Lovat, the chief of the clan, surrounded by seven strawberry leaves.

Sir Walter Raleigh who, in addition to making his name by throwing his cloak into a mud puddle for Queen Elizabeth I to step on and keep her feet dry, was also responsible for bringing tobacco to England and starting off the entire cigarette industry, and may well have been one of those who brought back the wild strawberry from Virginia. He certainly devised another use for the berries than merely enjoying them in a bowl with cream.

"Take a gallon of Strawberries," he wrote, "and put them in a pint of aqua vitae (brandy). Let them stand four or five days, strain them gently out and sweeten the water as you please with fine sugar."

Like several of our local home wine makers today, he didn't believe in the aging process.

YARROW

A great deal, my liege, depends
On having clever bards for friends.
What had Achilles been without his Homer?
A tailor, woolen-draper or a comber!
John Wolcot, A Moral Reflection to George III

Homer told us that Chiron, a great physician in Greek mythology, also happened to be a centaur, half man-half horse. He was also a teacher of all subjects and skills which a future hero of Athens might need, including the skill of archery. When he died, Zeus sent him into the heavens to become the constellation of stars known as The Archer, Sagittarius, which is why that sign of the Zodiac is still represented by a centaur with a drawn bow in his hands.

One of Chiron's star pupils was Achilles, who went on to become a hero of the Trojan Wars. Not only did Chiron teach him archery, but he also put on his other hat and taught the youth medicine, particularly how to treat war wounds by using a certain plant as a poultice. This knowledge, however, did not help Achilles himself very much. He fully believed that his mother, Thetis, after whom one of our local islands is named, had made him impervious to wounds by dipping him in the River Styx. He failed to realize that she had held him by one ankle to do so and that the one heel never actually got into the water. So, when Paris eventually shot him in the same heel with an arrow, Achilles did not bother to treat himself with Chiron's remedy. Blood poisoning set in and he died. And the plant which he failed to use was named *Achillea* after him.

One of the most obvious characteristics of this plant is that the leaves are so finely divided that it looks as though there are thousands of them. This gave rise to the second part of the botanic name, *millefolium*, meaning a thousand leaves, and to the corruption of that words which has created one of the plant's common names, milfoil. *Achillea millefo-*

53

lium is also known by many other names, some of them originating from the plant's ability to stop a wound from bleeding and from its antiseptic qualities. Soldier's wound wort, carpenter's weed and nose-bleed were all names commonly used in England. But the origin of the name most commonly used today, Yarrow, is uncertain. The Old English version of it, as long ago as the year 725, was 'gearwe,' which seems to have had no meaning other than as the name of the plant. A river in Scotland called the Yarrow may be named that because the flower grows along its banks, but that's about as far as one can go in trying to trace where the name came from.

Yarrow is a very common wildflower in this area, growing on road sides, in fields and in gardens, wherever it can get full sunshine. Apart from the distinctive leaves, which, incidentally, have an equally distinctive and pleasant scent, the flower head differs from nearly all of the other mop-headed plants growing here, in that, unlike them, since the yarrow is a member of the Compositae or daisylike family, each of the tiny flowers which make up the head are like individual miniature daisies. A variety with pinkish petals is not uncommon and there are also several escapees from local gardens, whose flowers range through the yellows and reds of the spectrum.

Probably because of its curative qualities, which, according to the herbalists, go far beyond the treatment of wounds to the relief of fevers and headaches, indigestion and chicken pox, yarrow was always associated with witchcraft, both the good and the bad varieties. But on balance, since the plant's power was evidently used for good, it was considered to bring good fortune and a bride who carried it in her wedding bouquet ensured for herself seven years of happiness.

ROSES

In the last month of May, I made her posies.
I heard her often say that she liked roses.
But she did all disdain and threw them back again,
Therefor 'tis flat and plain! Phillida flouts me.

Anonymous sixteenth-century poet

Forty million years ago, as the earth shook, the sky filled with smoke
and what are now the islands of the Georgia Basin heaved themselves
up from the bottom of a prehistoric sea, volcanic dust settled gently on
a wild rose, blooming on a hillside in Colorado, pressing and preserving
it, gently turning it into stone. In the Museum of the Rose, near Paris,
its fossilized remains are there in a glass case for all to see, along with
those of even older roses, some of them identifiable as species which
still bloom today, unchanged after all those millennia.

Thirty nine million, nine hundred and ninety-five thousand years or so
later, *Homo sapiens*, who had not even existed when the Colorado rose
blossomed and died, taught themselves how to write. Among the earliest words, scratched into the remains of a clay tablet found in the ruins
of Babylon, where King Nebuchadnezzar built his Hanging Gardens,
is the name of the rose. From the very beginnings of civilization, roses
and the human race have grown hand in hand.

There is no country in the Northern Hemisphere which does not have
its native rose. From Greenland to Ethiopia, from Siberia to Mexico
the long way round, everywhere one travels, wild roses grow. How many
different species there are, no one knows for sure. Some botanists say
three hundred, others count half that number, but these are totally
separate species of roses which they are talking about, not just different
varieties which number in the thousands, nor does it include the many
relatives in the huge Rosaceae family—apples and pears, cherries,
blackberries and so on.

Here in the Northwest, since settled down from all of that earlier
upheaval, the Nootka rose, *Rosa nutkana*, has become our more common native species. It got that name because it was first seen by
Europeans when Captain Cook arrived at Nootka Sound on Vancouver
Island in 1778. The other native local rose is the dwarf woodland rose,
also known as the baldhip rose, which is an accurate translation of the

botanic name, *Rosa gymnocarpa*. The Nootka rose is by far the larger of the two, both in the size of flower and of the entire plant also. It is very common along our road sides, often mixed in with other roses which have naturalized themselves here, after having been brought initially by settlers. Of these non-native roses, the dog rose is the most frequently seen and it can be differentiated easily from the native ones by its having thorns hooked like a dog's tooth, whereas the Nootka rose's thorns are straight.

Dozens, perhaps hundreds, of books have been written about roses since that old Babylonian scribe started the trend. Hardly a single poet, in any language, has failed to mention them as symbols of love. But the greatest honor which mankind could bestow on any plant, comes to the rose through the derivation of a single word, common to many languages. In ancient Persia, rose gardens were called *paridaeza*. We call that 'paradise.'

SWEET CICELY

First let me tell you whence her name has sprung,
Cecilia, meaning as the books agree,
Lily of Heaven in our English tongue,
To signify her chaste virginity.
Chaucer, Canterbury Tales, Second Nun's Prologue

The Second Nun

Coeli lilia, Lily of Heaven, may possibly have been the source of the name of this second-century martyr, as Chaucer says. But on the other hand, she was a Sicilian and the coincidence between name and nationality is rather hard to ignore completely.

Cecilia was a young virgin, living and dying in the second century. For refusing to give up her belief in Christ, she was boiled for two days and, when she was still alive after that, an executioner tried to cut off her head with a sword. Three blows to the neck failed to sever it and she was left to bleed to death, which she eventually did. She was later canonized as Saint Cecelia and, since somewhere along the line she was thought to have invented the organ as a musical instrument, she became the patron saint of music. Her saint's day is November 22, and one can be certain that every year on that day, someone will play some of the music composed in her honor on CBC Radio, such as Benjamin Britten's "Hymn to St. Cecilia" with words by W. H. Auden:

Blessed Cecilia, appear in visions
To all musicians, appear and inspire;
Translated daughter, come down and startle
Composing mortals with immortal fire!

Two very similar plants have been named after this saint. The first of these, which grows wild in Europe and is cultivated in many of our local herb gardens over here, is the *Myrris odorata*. The second, which is a native to this region, is the *Osmorhiza chilensis* and, as the second word there implies, it is native to Chile too and was first identified there. The common name for both of these plants is sweet cicely, a herb whose roots, boiled and chopped like the saint herself, were said by the English herbalist, John Gerard to be "very good for old people that are dull and without courage; it rejoiceth and comforteth the heart and increaseth their lust and strength."

Our local sweet cicely grows to about two feet tall, with pale green, quite deeply notched leaves divided into three leaflets and clusters of tiny white flowers at the top of the stems, similar to those of the parsley and carrot family to which it is related. It is also, however, related to the highly poisonous hemlock and, as with all wild plants, one ought to be absolutely sure of one's identifications before trying to eat them.

The botanic name *Osmorhiza* comes from two Greek words, *osme* meaning sweet and *rhiza* meaning a root, for the roots of sweet cicely give off a definite anise-flavored sweetness and can be used to replace some of the sugar in cooked desserts such as rhubarb tarts. In France, the seeds of the European species are crushed and added to brandy to take the edge off the harshness.

Medicinally, sweet cicely has had few benefits attached to it, other than as a mild tonic or to treat flatulence. Most of the famous herbalists spent time warning readers not to mistake some other dangerous plant for this one, and I have fallen into the same trap.

INDIAN MUSTARD

And in the vats of Luna,
This year, the must shall foam
Round the white feet of laughing girls,
Whose sires have marched to Rome.

Macaulay, Lays of Ancient Rome

Those who make their own wine or, for that matter regularly indulge in solving crossword puzzles, know that 'must' is new wine and also the juice which the feet of those girls were pressing from the grapes at the village of Luna. The Latin word for it was *mustus*. If one crushes the seeds of a certain plant and mixes them into a paste with mustus, one ends up with a fiery hot must, a *mustus ardens* in Latin, and if one shortens that a little, a 'mustard.' That's where the word came from.

The plants which produce these seeds are members of the Brassica family, which includes cabbages, broccoli and turnips among others. All of these in turn are part of a much larger family, the Cruciferae or crosslike plants, which are so-named because their flowers have only four petals, forming a sort of Maltese cross.

Several Cruciferae family members grow locally, but the mustards are represented mainly by three types: the *Brassica campestris* or field mustard, which has become the self-seeding pest which its name sounds like; the *Brassica kaber*, commonly called charlock; and the *Brassica juncea*, known either as brown mustard or Indian mustard. The word *juncea* comes from the Latin word *juncus*, which means a rush plant, whose brown seeds are the same color as those of the brown mustard and also, incidentally, as the shoulder feathers of that common little brown bird, the junco.

Brown mustard grows to a height of about two feet, with branched stems and several bright yellow crosslike flowers. It is found on road sides and in ground which has been cultivated at some time in the past. It was originally imported from Europe and it is now cultivated as the source of most of the mustard seeds which are used commercially.

On the subject of commercial mustards, it was a Mrs. Clements of Durham in England, who, in the eighteenth century, perfected a method of grinding mustard seeds into a fine powder, which could be kept dry for long periods until it was mixed with water, wine or vinegar for use at the table. If one looks at a can of Keen's mustard, which is made in England and used to be called Colman's mustard, since it is produced by Reckitt and Colman, Ltd., one sees that they have been in business since 1742. This is the same mustard as that from which Mrs. Clement made her fortune.

 If one tastes a mustard seed, it is not at all hot or spicy on the tongue. This is because the seed contains an enzyme, which must be wetted in order to become active, whereupon it combines with an other constituent of the seed to form the hot taste which one associates with mustard. In confirmation of this, the directions on the Keen's can say to let the mixed mustard stand for ten minutes before use to allow the flavor to develop. That's why Mrs. Clements wanted to find a way to crush the seeds so finely that this chemical reaction would be maximized and the mustard able to reach its full flavor potential.

The famous Roman naturalist, Pliny the Elder, who lived at the time of Christ, listed in his books no less than forty recipes in which mustard was an ingredient. But fashions in food, like those in clothes, come and go, and by 1640, John Parkinson, another English herbalist, was writing about mustard that, "Our ancient forefathers, even the better sorts were not sparing in the use hereof, but nowadays it is seldom used by their successors being the clown's sauce and not fit for their tables." The fashion has changed once more and the seal on the Keen's can now reads, "By appointment to Her Majesty, Queen Elizabeth II, Manufacturers of Mustard...."

It was a close relative of our local mustard, the black mustard, which grows wild in Israel, reaching heights of ten to twelve feet, with strong branching stems, which gave us one of the Bible's best-known passages:

> The Kingdom of Heaven is like to a grain of mustard seed, which a man took and sowed in his field; which indeed is the least of all seeds, but when it is grown, it is the greatest among herbs and becometh a tree, so that the birds of the air come and lodge in the branches thereof.

GOOSEBERRIES

From the lone shieling of the misty island
Mountains divide us and the waste of seas.
Yet still the blood is strong, the heart is Highland,
And we in dreams behold the Hebrides.'

John Galt, The Canadian Boat Song

A little piece of Canadian history to start with. The city of Guelph, Ontario, was founded in 1827 by the man whose poem is quoted above. He was sent to Canada as a member of a British government commission, set up to find ways to compensate residents of Upper Canada for losses which they had sustained in the War of 1812.

This was achieved eventually through the establishment of the Canada Company which, for the sum of £348,680, purchased more than two million acres of Crown land northwest of the city of Hamilton and contracted to build towns there, construct roads and bridges and bring in a large number of settlers to fight off any future Yankee invasions. Part of the price paid to the Crown for the land went to pay off the war claims.

Another of the towns which the Canada Company founded was named Galt in honor of the Scottish commission member. Galt's son, Alexander, went on to become the first minister of finance in the new Dominion Parliament after confederation and later, the first Canadian high commissioner to London.

When are we getting to gooseberries? Right now.

A few months ago, I was reading John Galt's best known novel, *The Annals of the Parish*, which is a year by year account of the goings on in a Scottish country parish, purportedly written by the minister of the parish church. In it is the comment that, as the sugar trade between the West Indies and port of Glasgow increased during the 1770s, and sugar became plentiful and far cheaper than it had been up to then, the country folk planted "grozets and berry bushes" among the cabbages in their kitchen gardens and started to make jam, something which only the rich had been able to afford until then.

That brought back the memory that in Scotland, a gooseberry is called a grozet. Like several other Scots words, it is a simple mispronuncia-

Goose-Berry

tion of a French word, probably brought to Scotland by Mary Queen of Scots, who had been married to the French king. That word is *grosseille*, which in turn comes from the Latin *grossularia*, which is the source of the botanical family name of Grossulariacae, which includes, not surprisingly after all this, gooseberries.

Our most common local wild gooseberry is the *Ribes lobbii*, the red-flowered gooseberry, but even so, it is not particularly plentiful. Its small, downward hanging red flowers, with white centers, look quite like miniature fuchsias and are followed by little green berries, which are rather bitter to taste. Although the lobed leaves are similar to those of other gooseberries and also those of their close relative, the currants, gooseberries can be identified by their having sharp spines along their stems. *Ribes*, by the way, comes from the Moorish name for a different plant altogether.

CLEAVERS

Therefore shall a man leave his father and his mother
and shall cleave unto his wife.
The Book of Common Prayer, Wedding Service

Nature invented Velcro long before man caught on. That, of course,
was the object of the whole thing. The seeds of certain plants are
covered with tiny hooks, which catch on the hair of passing animals,
causing the seeds to leave parent plants and cleave (stick) to their new
partner. Without wishing to stretch the marriage metaphor too far, the
seed later gets brushed off somewhere along the road and is left to
germinate and multiply on its own. From all this came the common
name for several similar plants, one of which grows freely in this part
of the world, cleavers.

Our local variety's botanic name is *Galium aparine*. *Galium* comes from
the Greek word for milk, for the version of the plant which grows in
many parts of Europe was crushed and added to milk in order to curdle
it in preparation for cheese making. But *Galiums* also have a pleasant,
mild scent and their stems are soft, so it was probably on account of
these characteristics that they were used by people as bedding material,
hence the other common name for the family, 'bedstraw.' The *Galium
verum*, the 'true' bedstraw, is generally known in England as lady's
bedstraw. Knowing how persistently its seeds stick to one's pant legs, it
is fairly easy to picture some medieval lady in her nightgown, smothered
from head to toe in little green seeds, looking like a human alligator.

Some of the perennial bedstraws were also important dye plants, their
roots being dug and boiled to produce a scarlet dye for wool.

Going back to the essay on gooseberries, the quotation at the top by
Galt referred to "the lone shieling of the misty islands." A shieling or
shiel, as it was also called, is a summer pasture, where animals are taken
to graze on the lush grasses. The "misty islands" are the Hebrides, off
the west coast of Scotland and on the shielings of these islands,
bedstraws grew in great profusion along the back of the beaches where
the pastures began. The women who tended the animals sheared their
sheep and spun their wool while they were out on the pastures and dug
the roots of the bedstraws to dye it. Unfortunately, the bedstraw roots
were binding the loose sand and once they were dug up, the sand began

63

to spread back into the pastures, threatening to destroy them. Because of this, one of the world's first pieces of environmental legislation was passed by the Scottish parliament, making it illegal to dig the roots. And to make sure that those who disobeyed the law did not become repeat offenders, the penalty for those found guilty was death.

Our *Galium aparine* is a weak-looking specimen, which trails along the ground. The stems, leaves and seeds are all covered by tiny hooks, which increase the likelihood of their catching on animals, for this is an annual plant which depends entirely on being reseeded for the coming year. The seeds, which develop after the clusters of small white flowers have faded, usually grow in pairs, tight together at the end of short stems. The pale green leaves grow in a circle or whorl around the stem, like pointed collars.

The Greek word *gala* relating to milk has no linguistic connection whatsoever with the Italian word *gala*, meaning a special occasion. There is, however, a coincidental link by way of the bedstraws.

Gala in Italian actually meant a brightly colored material, which was used to make party dresses. One went to the party 'in gala,' in the same way as one might go in costume or in uniform. The party itself then became a 'gala occasion,' like a formal-wear occasion or a black-tie dinner. Now the affair itself has become a gala.

When Elizabeth I was Queen of England, she became fascinated by Italian social fashions and brought in Italian dancing-masters and Italian-type parties at which the guests all dressed up in gala. This created a demand for the special cloth needed for the party clothes and one small group of Scottish countrywomen took advantage of this opportunity. When they went to the shiels for the summer, they dyed and spun the thread there, which they then used to weave the gala cloth. This happened in the south of Scotland, in the border hills where the law about digging bedstraw roots did not apply, so the scarlet dye could be produced legally. These shiels became known as the gala shiels and from the industry started there by those few women has grown one of Britain's main centers of cloth manufacture, the town of Galashiels.

HONEYSUCKLE

Come into the garden, Maude,
I am here at the gate alone,
And the woodbine spices are wafted abroad
And the musk of the rose is blown.

Alfred, Lord Tennyson, Maude

That is quoted because of the third line, the bit about the "woodbine spices," although for some people the whole verse might bring back memories of the Victorian ballad which used these lines, which was a popular after-dinner piece for would-be lyric tenors.

Woodbine is one of the common names for the plant which is more usually known as a honeysuckle, of which two different varieties grow around here. These are the orange honeysuckle, *Lonicera ciliosa*, and the purple honeysuckle, *Lonicera hispidula*. Both of these are vines and are excellent climbers, for their flowers can often be seen blooming far up a roadside tree. The purple variety, however, also seems to be happy trailing along the ground, twining in among the trailing blackberries and salal.

The leaves of all honeysuckles grow in pairs, opposite each other at regular intervals along the plant's woody stems. It was its tendency to bind itself to other species which gave it its earlier name of woodbinde, which later evolved into the present form. Honeysuckle was first applied to clover and refers to the sweet taste of the flowers if one sucks upon them, but at some stage clover stopped being called that and the name moved across to the woodbines. *Lonicera* comes from the name of a sixteenth-century German physician, Adam Lonitzer. The second parts of the two botanic names refer to particular aspects of the hairs which grow on the leaves and stems of the plants.

Back again to Maude. If that young woman had let herself be talked into coming out to the garden in this area, one in which only the native species grew, she would have been in for a bit of a disappointment, for neither of our honeysuckles wafts any spices at all abroad. They are both completely scentless. And this is because nature is smart and these varieties don't need a scent. Because of the long, tubular shape of the flowers, and the fact that the nectar is right down at the bottom of the tubes, only a creature with a long, narrow tongue can get far enough

65

inside to reach it and pollinate the plant at the same time. In this region, that creature is the hummingbird, which is attracted to the plant in daylight by the bright color of the petals and is totally disin-

terested in sweet scents. In England, where the poem was written, there are no hummingbirds and the only creatures with long enough tongues to get down inside the European honeysuckles are certain moths. Moths have a very strong sense of smell and prefer to do most of their flying at night, when predators can't see them and when all flowers, like cats, look gray. So to attract these moths to their flowers, these European varieties of honeysuckle have developed a very sweet scent, which reaches its greatest strength in the coolness of the night, wafting its spices abroad.

So here we have that poet, the son of a rector, forty-six years old at the time that he wrote the poem, calling on young Maude, whom he admits was "not seventeen" even, to come out to the garden gate in the dark and smell the honeysuckle. You've got to watch out for these chaps.

COLUMBINE

Gardener. 'The weeds that his broad spreading leaves did shelter...
Are pluck'd up root and all by Bolingbroke;
I mean, the Earl of Wiltshire, Bushy, Green.'
First servant. 'What! are they dead?'
Gardener. 'They are.'

Shakespeare, Richard II

In July 1399, William Scrope, Earl of Wiltshire and his fellow con-
spirators, Sir John Bushy and Sir Henry Greene, were hanged for
treason from the battlements of the city of Bristol. Six years later,
Richard le Scrope, Archbishop of York, was arrested for armed insur-
rection and beheaded in his own cathedral town. The only male family
member who seems to have survived this slaughter of Scropes was
Richard, Baron Scrope of Bolton, who had served as lord chancellor in
the past but whose interests during the danger period were largely tied
up in a law suit against Sir Robert Grosvenor, whom he accused of
improperly using his coat of arms. The suit took five years in the courts
to complete, one of the longest in English legal history, and Baron
Richard won his case.

Thus ended the Scrope family's brief appearance in history, but the
name crops up again once more, a hundred years later, in a poem by
John Skelton, addressed to a beautiful young lady, Mistress Jane
Scrope, whom he describes as "a daisy delectable, a columbine commendable."

We have a fairly commendable columbine of our own growing wild on
the West Coast, the western columbine or *Aquilegia formosa*. It flowers,
usually beside the road, in late May and early June, growing to a height
of about two feet or a little more. The stems, which branch near the
top, carry nodding coral red and yellow flowers. The main leaves, which
are deeply divided around their margins, grow from the bottom of the
stems, although smaller leaves of the same shape appear higher up. The
shape of the flower is almost impossible to describe and this is most
definitely a case where a picture is worth far more than a thousand
words.

In the distant past, someone with a much stronger imagination than
most of us decided that the flower looked like several pigeons clustered

together. The Latin word for a pigeon or dove was *columba*, so that was used as the source of the plant's common name, the columbine, and also of course, of British Columbia eventually.

Columbine

When it came to giving the plant a botanic name, however, a different bird came to mind. From some supposed resemblance to the talons of an eagle, *aquilla* in Latin, the name *aquilegia* was assigned to it. Or so some say. Another theory suggests that, because a watery nectar often hangs in droplets from the tips of the petals, the plant was called a water-carrier in Latin, this being derived from *aqua* meaning water and *legere*, to carry. Take your pick, if it matters.

As for the second word, *formosa*, it has nothing to do with the island which once bore that name, which we now call Taiwan. The word actually means beautiful in a shapely sense, a description which could have been applied, one assumes, to Mistress Jane Scrope.

WATERCRESS

Gillyflowers and Watercresses
For her senses, Nettie grows,
Scent her very soul caresses,
Taste, which wrinkles up her nose.

Miles Macrae, Trivia

Take the Latin words *tortium*, meaning distortion or twisting and *nasi*, meaning nasal or of the nose, join them together in reverse order and make a slight spelling change and you end up with a common garden flower, the nasturtium. But what does it have to do with twisting noses? Nothing at all. That's because what we all call a nasturtium isn't a nasturtium. It's a *Tropaeolum majus*, a native of Peru, and neither the country nor the plant had even been discovered by Europeans when the Romans started to call a local herb a 'nasitortium.'

The real and original nasturtium, the *Nasturtium officinale*, is nothing more than our common or garden watercress, which was introduced to North America by settlers and which now happily grows wild in creeks and ditches throughout our area. And it was the pungent, rather peppery taste of the leaves which apparently caused some of those who ate it to wrinkle their noses, thereby giving the plant its name.

The common name 'cress' comes from the word 'cross,' because this is one of the members of the same family as the mustards, the Cruciferae, whose four-petalled flowers form the shape of a cross. The 'water' part of the name distinguishes this particular cress from others on the basis of its preference for growing where there is running water covering its roots.

Watercress is fairly easy to identify. It forms a dense mat of small, dark green leaves and its little branches are tipped in summer by clusters of the tiny, white, four-petalled flowers, which are followed by seed pods of up to an inch in length. A plant like this, growing in a wet location, with peppery-tasting leaves is probably watercress.

This is a plant which is full of things that are good for us—vitamins A, B_2, C, D, E, iron, phosphorus, calcium—so it is hardly surprising that the word *officinale* appears in its botanic name, signifying that the plant was recognized to have medicinal value, particularly of course, as part of the treatment of anyone who was suffering from a deficiency of any of these constituents.

Since watercress is also very tasty and needs no preparation other than a quick wash, it has always been a popular food item. This led to its becoming a commercially cultivated crop and by about the year 1800, Richard Brook was able to write in his *Cyclopaedia of Botany* that, "the quantity used in the neighbourhood of London is truly astonishing. Every morning throughout the year, although there are something like two millions of inhabitants, they all have water-cresses within call and can have them to breakfast if they choose."

Young women, bearing baskets full of watercress, hawked it through the streets of London in the early morning, buying their supplies at dawn from the huge hampers of it brought into town from the surrounding areas during the night and sold beside the railings at Farringdon Market.

So why was the Peruvian *Tropeolum* called a nasturtium? Just because its seeds have a slightly similar taste to watercress—no better reason than that.

DAME'S VIOLET

It was the schooner Hesperus
That sailed the wintry sea;
And the skipper had taken his little daughter,
To bear him company.

Longfellow, The Wreck of the Hesperus

The derivation of language really does make an interesting study. Take our word 'west,' for example, since that's where we live. It comes to us through Old German from the Latin word *vesper*, meaning evening, or the direction in which the sun sets. *Vesper* in turn comes from a Greek word, *hesperos*, which means the same thing. Both *vesper* and *hesperos* were also names given by the Romans and the Greeks to what they thought was a bright star, which often shone in the evening sky. We now call that same object the planet Venus. And Longfellow named his poetic schooner after it.

The evening services in most of the Christian churches were called vespers and Edward Gibbon, who became famous through his great work, *The Decline and Fall of the Roman Empire*, remarked that "It was at Rome, on the 15th of October, 1764, as I sat musing amidst the ruins of the Capitol, while the barefoot friars were singing vespers in the Temple of Jupiter, that the idea of writing the decline and fall of the city first started to my mind."

Hundreds of years before Longfellow, but at least 500 years after the founding of Rome (which tradition says was done by Romulus in 753 B.C.), the Greek philosopher Aristotle died and in his will, left his garden to his favourite pupil, Theophrastus. Wandering through the garden in the evening, Theophrastus noticed that one of the plants growing there produced a stronger scent as darkness fell and gave to that plant the name 'hesperos'. That name crossed to

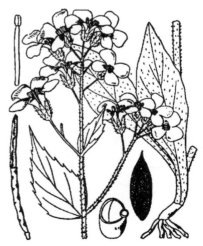

Rome where, in Latin, it became *'hesperis'* and in the first century A.D., the Roman naturalist Pliny, seeing how popular the plant had become with ladies, started calling it the ladies' hesperis or *Hesperis matronalis*, and that is still its botanic name today. Its English common name, dame's violet, continues the idea of its being a favourite plant of women and also tells us the color of its flowers, but it is not, technically speaking, a violet. The Maltese cross shape of the four-petalled flower gives the clue and this plant, like mustard and cress before it, is a Cruciferae.

Dame's violet grows fairly plentifully in the Northwest, often by the road, and reaches a height of between two and three feet, depending on the conditions where it is growing. There are good reasons why so many of our wildflowers choose to live beside the roads. There are often ditches and these, being designed to collect rain water runoff, are frequently damper than the surrounding land, which suits most plants. In addition, the clearing of trees to build the road lets light in to help the plants to develop. In country districts, passing loads of hay can drop seeds from other places which fall by the road and germinate there. So a road side can be almost an ideal place for many plants to live, so long as the local highways crew is not too enthusiastic with its grass cutting or spraying programs.

And in case some readers are not familiar with Longfellow's poem, there are two lines later on which, with the exercise of a little imagination, guide one to the rest of the sad story:

> The Father answered not a word,
> A frozen corpse was he.

WOOLLY SUNFLOWER

No, the heart that has truly lov'd never forgets,
But as truly loves on to the close,
As the Sunflower turns on her god, when he sets,
The same look which she turn'd when he rose.
Thomas Moore, Irish Melodies

The greater Sun-floure

An interesting phenomenon, common to many plants, is a tendency for the top of the stem, whether it be a growing tip or a flower, to follow the sun on its course across the sky from dawn to dusk. Vines in particular make use of this capacity as they grow upwards. One can see this in action quite clearly in a vegetable garden, where the tall varieties of beans twist themselves around a string or pole, gaining support while they reach toward the sun.

As the poet pointed out, one of the plants which turns its head to the sun in this manner is the sunflower. Although there are several different plants commonly called sunflowers of one sort or another, the only one which grows wild in our area is the woolly sunflower, the *Eryophyllum lanatum*. The common sunflower from which oil is produced commercially and whose seeds are favorites of birds and people alike, prefers the weather to the east of the Cascade Mountains and leaves this side alone.

The woolly sunflower usually grows on poor and rocky soil at the higher elevations on the San Juans and Gulf Islands and above the tree line on the mainland. It is low growing, as one might expect from a plant which lives in windy and exposed locations. Its flowers are bright canary yellow, two inches across, with a slightly darker center. Its leaves are deeply indented and divided and look gray and woolly because of being covered by tiny hairs. This was the reason why the plant was given its

73

botanic name, from the Greek words *erion* meaning wool and *phyllon* meaning a leaf. And just in case someone failed to get the message, the Latin word *Lanatum*, meaning woolly, was tacked on for good measure, giving us a woolly, woolly leaf.

Never having stood for hours watching a woolly sunflower, I have to admit that I don't know if its flowers follow the sun or not. But even John Gerard had the same problem 400 years ago, when he wrote, "Some have reported it to turn with the sun, which I could never observe, although I have endeavoured to find out the truth of it."

Then there are those other plants which, for some unknown reason, probably pure perverseness, turn in the opposite direction. Michael Flanders and Donald Swan put it quite succinctly,

> The fragrant Honeysuckle spirals clockwise to the sun,
> And many other creepers do the same.
> But some climb anti-clockwise, the Bindweed does for one,
> Or Convolvulus, to give its proper name.

MONKEY FLOWERS

A fig for those by law protected!
Liberty's a glorious feast!
Courts for cowards were erected,
Churches built to please the priest.
                    Robert Burns, Love and Liberty

Until the year 1710, the *Church of England Prayer Book* contained a form of service to be used on those occasions when the king or queen reached out and touched the swollen lymph glands on the necks of those of their loyal and trusting subjects, who had come to be cured by this royal touch of "The King's Evil." The ceremony continued on for a while beyond that date, though, for in 1712, Samuel Johnson, the future compiler of the first English dictionary, was taken by his mother to London to be touched by Queen Anne, for he "had the misfortune to be much afflicted by the Scrofula, or King's Evil." Presumably either her Majesty's touch or the prayers were successful, for he lived on for seventy-two more years.

Staying with the medical theme for a moment, swollen lumps at the other end of the torso were equally common. These went by the common names of 'pyles' or 'figs.' Now there were obvious limits to the extent of touching which royalty could be expected to perform, so a different treatment had to be devised for this other unfortunate condition. At that time, many physicians believed in the Doctrine of Signatures, the theory that diseases could be treated by using plants, or parts of plants, which resembled the affected flesh. There was one particular plant whose roots were covered with swollen lumps. By coincidence, before this rather weird theory arose, this plant had been called by the Romans, *cervicaria*, because they had used it in the treatment of neck or cervical problems. But a lump was a lump, at the neck or at the other end and as a result of the plant being used to treat both sorts, it began to be known either as the *scrophularia* or the fig wort.

Various members of the fig wort family grow wild in our area, the best known of these probably being the foxglove. But another cousin, which is just about as abundant, is the monkey flower, whose little yellow face was thought to look so monkeylike that it got that name. Its botanic name, *Mimulus*, means a mimic, again because the flower mimics a funny face.

Three different varieties of monkey flower grow on the islands and a fourth, with red flowers, appears elsewhere in this region. *Mimulus guttatus*, the common monkey flower is, as its name implies, the most common and also the largest. It can often be found in ditches and damp places from July onwards. *Guttatus* means speckled and refers to the reddish purple spots which appear on many of this flower's lower lips. It has a tiny sister, the *Mimulus alsinoides* or little monkey flower, which is only one or two inches tall and is one of the earliest of our spring flowers, generally appearing on grassy slopes near the sea or springing from cracks in the cliffs where it sets seed and disappears before the droughts of summer overtake it. *Alsinoides* just means that it looks a bit like another flower, a form of chickweed, which was once known as alsine. The third yellow-flowered version is the *Mimulus moschatus* or musk flower. David Douglas found it growing here and sent seeds back to his employers at the Royal Horticultural Society in 1828. It quickly gained popularity, both as a garden plant and as a house plant, because of its pleasant musky scent. However, a funny thing happened around the turn of the century. All over Europe and North America, wherever the musk flower grew, either wild or in cultivation, it lost its scent and a hundred years later, it has never come back.

And if you "don't give a fig" about that, you now realize that it's not a piece of fruit that you're talking about.

TEASEL

Sable, a Chevron Ermine, between two Habicks in chief, and a
Tessel in base, proper.
Guillim, Heraldry

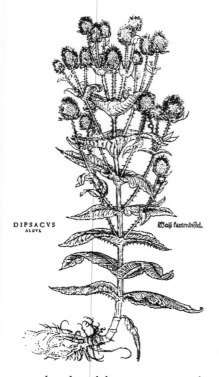

DIPSACVS
ALUVL

Wciß kartembiſel.

If that makes no sense at all, it is
hardly surprising, for it is a description of Armorial bearings, or a
Heraldic shield, written in the year
1660 in the peculiar language of
Heraldry.

It can be translated roughly as saying that the shield is black, with a
white chevron across it with its
point uppermost, two cloth working tools called habicks in the upper third, on each side of the
chevron's point and a teasel flower,
in its correct colors, at the foot. It
describes the arms of the Worship-
ful Company of Cloth Workers,
which used to be one of the leading
trade guilds of London.

The relevant part of this for us is
the natural-colored teasel, for this
tall, prickly plant is now one of our
many imported wildflowers, reach-
ing a height of five or even six feet. Its connection with cloth workers
lies in the sharp little hooks which cover the flower head when it dries.
Wooden forms filled with these heads were used in the final preparation
of woolen cloth to comb up the nap of the fabric and give it softness
and fluffiness.

The name teasel comes from an Old English word *taesan*, meaning to
pull apart. And this word was applied to the act of separating and
splitting the ends of wool fibers to create softness. We now use the word
most frequently in the form of "teasing out" knots from one's hair. The
other common meaning of the verb to tease, referring to imposing some

petty annoyance upon somebody, derived from the same idea of picking something apart, but is a fairly modern use of the word, not more than 400 years old.

As for the plant's botanic name, our local variety is the *Dipsacus sylvestris*. The first word comes from the Greek *dipsao*, meaning to thirst, which is also where our word for a heavy drinker, a dipsomaniac, comes from. This seems to be an allusion to the fact that rain and dew accumulate in the cuplike bases of the leaves of the teasel as though the plant was constantly collecting water to slake its thirst. The second word means that this is a plant of the woods, but although that may be where it prefers to grow in its native Europe, here it tends to appear in more open and sunny locations. The flower head itself is made up of hundreds of small blue flowers, which cluster together to form what looks almost like a thistle head.

Soon after that description of the shield was written in a book about Heraldry, the great fire of London destroyed the cloth-workers' meeting place. Samuel Pepys, whose diaries are among the most fascinating and amusing of English social commentaries, wrote in his journal on September 6, 1666, that he had been that day "to see Cloth-workers' Hall on fire these three days and nights. It was pretty to see how hard the women did work in the cannells (gutters) sweeping of water, but then they would scold for drink and be as drunk as devils. I saw good butts of sugar broke open in the street and people go and take handfuls out and put into beer and drink it." That was probably a highly effective way to revive exhausted fire fighters, but for some reason our local fire authorities no longer appear to recommend it.

Things just ain't what they used to be.

BLACK NIGHTSHADE

The kiss of the sun for pardon,
The song of the birds for mirth,
One is nearer God's Heart in a garden
Than anywhere else on earth.

Dorothy Frances Gurney, God's Garden

The Latin word for the sun is *sol*. That's where our word 'solar' comes from, as in solar energy, which provides us with warmth and comfort. Another word for comfort is solace, so it is fairly logical that something else which provides a form of comfort in the relief of pain should also become associated with the sun. It was for this reason that strongest and most effective of the narcotic plants known to the Romans was given the name *solanum*.

These days, all of the closely related family members of that plant are grouped together in the *Solanum* genus and undoubtedly the one which everybody knows best, although probably not as a *Solanum*, is the *Solanum tuberosum*, whose tubers most of us eat almost every day, calling them potatoes. Second only to that would be the *Solanum lycopersicum*, the tomato, and probably the third best known, by name if not by usage, is the *Solanum belladonna*, the deadly nightshade.

The deadly nightshade is the source of the narcotics which gave comfort to the Romans. Unfortunately it also killed a lot of them, for it is, as John Gerard said, "a plant so furious and deadly." It is so much so, in fact, that Abraham Tucker, writing in about 1735, commented that even "Apothecaries, when dispensing a recipe wherein antimony, solanum, laudanum or mercury is an ingredient, are extremely careful." With that list, one would certainly hope so.

However, deadly nightshade also has its virtues. Roman ladies (*donna*) put drops of the juice which they squeezed from the berries into their eyes, so that their pupils became dilated. They believed that this made them look more beautiful (*bella*).

79

This was where the second part of the botanic name, *belladonna*, came from. Eye doctors still use the substance contained in the juice which has this dilating effect. It is now known as 'Atropine' and it is among the most effective antidotes to many of the dangerous insecticides being used around the world. Since many of those are derivatives from the nerve gas developed by the Nazis during World War II, atropine is also issued to troops who are in danger of a nerve gas attack.

Deadly nightshade does grow in this area, although it is not very common. There is far more of its cousin, the black nightshade, *Solanum nigrum*. One often finds this in gardens, where it sprawls along the ground, its thin stems growing to a length of about two feet. The flowers grow in clusters along the stem, white, with deep yellow centers and these are followed by small, green berries, which gradually turn to red, then to black as they ripen. These black berries are what gave the plant its name, and there is some disagreement as to whether or not they are poisonous. To be on the safe side, however, it is probably better to follow the advice given by John Gerard in respect to the deadly nightshade, "Banish it from your gardens."

And just to round things off, the name of the drug atropine comes from Greek mythology. Three of Zeus' daughters, collectively known as the Fates, were thought to determine the destiny of every human being. The first, Clothos, spins the thread of life. The second, Lachesis, winds it onto a spool, and when the thread has reached its appointed length for each and every one of us, Atropos cuts it off.

CLOVER

With spots quadrangular of di'mond form'
Ensanguined hearts, clubs typical of strife
And spades, the emblem of untimely graves.
William Cowper, The Winter Evening

Did you ever stop and wonder why the suit of clubs in a pack of cards
is represented by a clover leaf? After all, a heart is a heart and even a
spade is a bit like the old-fashioned pointed spades which were used in
the middle ages. But to use a clover leaf for a club seems to make very
little sense.

Well, it all came about because of Hercules or Heracles, as the Greeks
called him. He was an illegitimate son of Zeus, the top god, and Zeus'
wife, Hera, took a bit of a dislike to the poor chap because of that. In
fact, she hated him so much that when he was older, she drove him mad
and made him murder all of his own five children, reckoning that he'd
be sure to hang for that and be out of her hair for ever.

However, the local king came up with a different sentence. He ordered
Hercules to perform twelve virtually impossible tasks and, if he completed them, he could then go free. This early form of community
service became known as "The Twelve Labours of Hercules" and most
of them consisted of ridding the neighbourhood of particularly nasty
and vicious beasts. Hercules was expected to provide his own weapons,
so he hauled a wild olive tree from the ground, hacked off its branches
and roots and used it as a club. Over the centuries, drawings of
Hercules and his club became fairly stylized on Greek pottery and the
club itself was generally shown as having three lumps on the end, where
the roots had been cut away.

The clover leaf is usually made up of three leaflets and the botanic
name of the plant, *Trifolium*, meaning three-leaved, reflects that. And
since these three leaves look quite like the old drawings of Hercules
club, the Latin name for a club, *clava*, became a common Roman name
for the plant. In time, the Dutch were calling it *klaver* and the English
changed this into clover.

So that's how the plant got its name and why clubs look like clover
leaves.

81

Many different types of clover grow around here, fifteen at least and undoubtedly several more. The most common of them is the white clover, *Trifolium repens*, which some city folk think of as a weed and try to eradicate from their lawns. Red clover, *Trifolium pratense*, would be the next most common, perhaps followed by a tall version called cow clover. But because there are so many of them, those who want to know what they all are will have to look in a guide book.

Clover has a long relationship with religion. It was venerated by the Druids, who saw in its trefoil leaves representations of the earth, the sea and the sky. To Christians, who often use the leaf shape in church windows and architectural embellishments, it represents the Trinity of Father, Son and Holy Spirit.

It was not until the year 1645, however, that clover was deliberately cultivated as an animal fodder. Sir Richard Weston of Sutton Manor in England planted the first recorded clover crop to feed his cattle and went on from there to plant the first field of turnips, for the same reason.

An interesting feature of red clover is that no insect, other than the honey bee, will pollinate it. So, when colonists took the seed to Australia where there were no wild honey bees, the crop totally failed and they had to import the bees to make sure that the next crop would produce its own seed for future years. Later on, of course, the Australians also imported rabbits, which love to eat clover and much else, and look where that got them.

PLANTAIN

Wheresoe'r they tread, beneath them
Springs a flower unknown among us,
Springs the White-man's Foot in blossom.
Longfellow, The Song of Hiawatha

There are many ways in which seeds can be spread from place to place, but only one plant, the plantain, seems to have been acknowledged for centuries to have traveled around the world on the soles of European feet. In fact the very name of this plant comes from the Latin word for the sole of a foot.

In a 1601 translation of Pliny's first-century *Natural History*, we can find plantain described as "a triviall and common hearbe, trodden under everie man's foot," but to be fair to him, Pliny then goes on to say that an even earlier author than himself, Themison, "a famous physician, sets forth a whole book of the hearbe...wherein he highly praiseth it."

The connection between plantains and feet continued through the centuries into the first recorded Anglo-Saxon common name for the plant, 'weibreode,' which means a broede or broad-leaved plant which grows by the wei or wayside. An incorrect translation of the Anglo-Saxon resulted in the plant sometimes being called 'waybread,' as though it were edible and by a further mistake, a tropical plant which is a close relative of the banana also became known as a plantain, even though as early as 1590, shortly after the tropical version had been found in South America, one of the leading naturalists of the time, Mendes da Costa, had written that the two plants were totally unconnected.

So if the common wayside plantain is of no use as food, why did Thomison praise it highly? Well, even the prestigious *New England Journal of Medicine* published an account of the use of crushed plantain leaves as an antidote to poison ivy. It has also been used to relieve insect stings and to heal wounds. Shakespeare's Romeo said that a plantain leaf was excellent for a broken shin and, according to John Gerard, "the juice dropped in the eies cooles the heate and inflammation thereof." Folk lore in Ireland and on the Isle of Man connects plantain with St. Patrick, who is said to have driven snakes from Ireland and it might

83

well have been this association that resulted in pieces of plantain root being carried in the pockets of settlers in America, to protect them from snake bites. From this belief, a second common name, 'snakeweed' arose, which is still used in some parts of the United States.

PLANTAGO
MAIOR.

There are three different members of the plantain in this area, *Plantago major*, which has the larger (major) leaf and is the broad-leaved variety which was called weibreod in the past; *Plantago lanceolata*, which means that the leaves are narrower and pointed-shaped, in fact, like a lance, which is what the Latin word means and whose common name is the ribwort plantain. That relates to the noticeable ribs or veins running lengthwise up the leaves. The seaside plantain, *Plantago maritima*, is common along the back of beaches and has grasslike leaves of up to a foot in length. The tiny white flowers on each of these are almost invisible against the long, brown, pistonlike seed heads. Driveways, paths, road verges and trails are all places where one can almost guarantee to find plantains. For, as Hiawatha nearly said, like Mary's little lamb, "everywhere the white man walked, the plantain's sure to grow."

ENCHANTER'S NIGHTSHADE

Circe prepared them a mixture of cheeses, barley-meal and
yellow honeys flavoured with Pramnian wine. But into this
dish she introduced a powerful drug....
Now, to all appearances they were swine; they had pigs' heads
and bristles and they grunted like pigs.

Homer, The Odyssey

There have been several news items recently about the use of an extract
from the bark of the Pacific yew tree, *Taxus brevifolia*, as an anticancer
drug known as taxol. And for centuries, people all over the world have
been chewing or brewing the bark of many varieties of willow trees to
relieve headaches. We now know that the factor in willow bark which
gives this reaction is a substance which was identified by a German
chemist, Beyer, and which is marketed under the names of ASA or
Aspirin.

At least 30 percent of the drugs approved for use in the U.S. and
Canada are derived from plants and, if there were some way in which
the large drug companies could patent wild plants, so that no competi-
tor could benefit from expensive research, many more plant-based
medicines would undoubtedly be discovered and there would probably
be some Native woman, somewhere in the world, who would say, "I told
you so!"

Another plant-based substance which has been in the news is evening
primrose oil, which practitioners of herbal medicine prescribe for both
external and internal disorders of various sorts. This comes from the
plant whose botanic name is *Oenothera biennis*. It does not appear in
the northern part of the West Coast but is quite common further south
and especially in Oregon. However several of its relatives, such as the
Clarkia which has been mentioned before, and fireweed, which everybody knows, are abundant.

On the subject of fireweed, which is native to the whole northern part
of the globe, most of the Aboriginal peoples in this area have always
considered it to be an essential part of their diet. It is interesting to
learn that in a comparison of the nutritional values of common domes-
tic fruits and vegetables carried out in 1974, it was discovered that, for
example, whereas 100 grams of spinach contained 8,100 International

Units of vitamin A, fireweed tested out at 18,708 IU and the same sort of superiority applied to vitamin C and other constituent nutrients. This type of evidence does make it a bit hard to accept that it is mere evolutionary coincidence that a plant so high in essential components grows in such great proliferation just where it is most needed by people and animals.

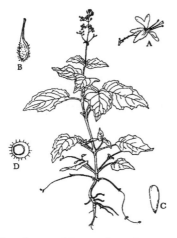

Another member of the same family is a rather delicate little plant, which grows in the shade of our local woods, the enchanter's nightshade or *Circea alpina*. Despite the second part of its common name, it has nothing whatever to do with the nightshade family, the Solanums. And the enchanter part is a minor mistake too, for this is said to have been the source of the "powerful drug" which Circe gave to Ulysses' crew and which turned them all into swine. Naturally enough, being the hero, Ulysses managed to get Mercury to show him the antidote, so that he could save his shipmates. Circe fell in love with him, bore him a son and, when he and his crew set off once more on their journey home, warned him about the Siren's song and suggested that they all plug their ears with wax when they were sailing past these ladies' island.

Now, if some big drug company had a bit of cash to spare, it might well find that enchanter's nightshade, like fireweed and evening primrose, contains something of medicinal importance. On the other hand, without having Mercury around on staff to help them out, they could end up with a laboratory full of pigs, and what would they do about that?

GREAT MULLEIN

To gild refined gold, to paint the lily,
To throw a perfume on the violet,
...or with a taper light
To seek the beauteous eye of heaven to garnish,
Is wasteful and ridiculous excess.

Shakespeare, King John

Continuing on from the enchanter's nightshade and the antidote to the drug which Circe gave to Ulysses' crew, it might be appropriate at this stage to identify it, for it is one of our local wildflowers too. This is what Homer had to say about it. "Then (Mercury) handed me a herb he had plucked from the ground and showed me what it was like.... The Gods call it 'Moly' and it is an awkward plant to dig up, at any rate for a mere man."

The gods called it 'moly' because it is *mollis*, which means soft, as in 'mollycoddle,' which an English dialect dictionary defined in 1903 as "a man who does household work," suggesting that he had it pretty soft. They should have tried it before they wrote that definition! And the part of the plant which feels particularly soft is its large woolly leaves, which is how one of its common names, donkey's ears, came about. Another common name arose because its stem, as well as the leaves, is hairy and absorbs oil so well that it could be dipped in tallow and used as a torch. Other common names arose from the connection with Circe's spells, witches' candle and hags' taper.

But apart from using it as a taper or to turn one's friends back from pigginess into looking like real people, moly had other uses. Smoking the dried leaves in a pipe was thought to be a remedy for asthma and, if one mixed the yellow flowers with lye, it would act as a hair bleach. Henry Coles, who was another of those English herbalists of the seventeenth century, wrote that "Husbandmen of Kent do give it their cattle against the cough of the lungs." As an infusion, it was used as a gargle to help tonsillitis and the leaves were pounded into a mush to relieve "figs or pyles."

And to identify it in modern terms, its present common name is great mullein, which comes from the old French name, Molleine, which in turn goes back to moly. The reason why it is great is simply because it

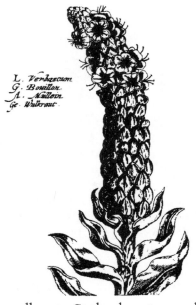

L. *Verbascum*
G. *Bonillon*
A. *Mullein*
Ge. *Walkraut*

can grow to almost eight feet tall. It is a biennial, a rosette of soft gray-green leaves forming during the first year of its life, followed the next year by the single tall stem, at the top part of which pale yellow flowers open at no set interval, sometimes above the earlier ones and sometimes below them. It produces huge quantities of seeds, which are very attractive to sparrows and finches, which can often be seen scratching around on the ground beneath this plant.

The botanic name is *Verbascum thapsus*. *Verbascum* is said to be a corruption of the Latin word for bearded, *barbatus*, because of the plant's hairiness and Thapsus was the name of a village in Sicily where it must have grown in some abundance. Back in the thirteenth century, it was actually called *Thapsus barbatus*.

If you want to put it to good use today, you could always use Pliny's suggestion of 2,000 years ago and wrap figs in it to prevent them from spoiling. That's the fruit sort of figs, of course.

SCARLET PIMPERNEL

We seek him here, we seek him there,
Those Frenchies seek him everywhere,
Is he in heaven? Is he in hell?
That demned, elusive Pimpernel?

Baroness Orczy

In the King James version of the New Testament, the First Letter of Peter is addressed to "the strangers scattered throughout Pontus." Pontus was a kingdom on the south shore of the Black Sea which, until about sixty years before the birth of Christ, had been ruled for a long time by King Mithradites. When he was a young man, the king had a physician whose name was Cravetas and who, in addition to having a broad knowledge of the herbal medicines of those days, was also a gifted artist and drew extremely accurate pictures of the plants which he used in his remedies.

Pontus was eventually overrun by a Roman army, which happened to have on its payroll its own army doctor, one Pedianus Dioscorides. This gentleman managed to lay his hands on Cratevas drawings, which would have been considered legitimate wartime loot. When he retired from the military, Dioscorides wrote a book, which he called *De Materia Medica*, or *Medical Matters* and used Cratevas' drawings to illustrate it. Although that original book has long since vanished, a copy of it made in the year 512 A.D. still exists in Vienna and there, among the pages, is a drawing of a plant with the name *Anagallis* written underneath, completely recognizable as the plant which is still known botanically today as *Anagallis arvensis* and whose common name is the scarlet pimpernel.

Of course the name scarlet pimpernel is possibly better known these days as that of a play, re-written into a book and then back into a screen play, which shows up every now and then on the late show, with Leslie Howerd in the lead role. The plant, however, is fairly widespread in the Pacific Northwest and is yet another of those European immigrants which have made this area their home.

This little annual flower sprawls along the ground and its half-inch wide, salmon red blooms start to blossom in late May. The small leaves, which are quite broad and some to a point at the tip, grow in pairs

89

opposite each other in a manner known as bipinnate. It has been suggested that this particular leaf arrangement resulted in the plant

Pimpernell

being originally known as the 'bipinnella,' and this name certainly appears in old books, but applied to a totally different plant. Over the years the name changed to 'pipinnella,' then 'pimpinnella' and by 1597, when Gerard was writing his herbal, to what we have today, the 'pimpernel.' But by that date, the name was being given to what we would now consider to be the proper plant. According to Gerard, its "juyce cures the toothach being snift up into the nosethrils."

The botanic name *Anagallis* is derived from the Latin verb *anagalere* meaning to make happy. If Dr. Cratevas succeeded in curing his royal master's toothache with scarlet pimpernel juice, one can accept that it might have made King Mithradites very happy indeed.

ROSE CAMPION

Geronte: 'It seems to me you are locating them wrongly; the heart is on the left and the liver is on the right.'
Sganarelle: 'Yes, in the old days that was so, but we have changed all that, and we now practise medicine by a completely new method.'

Molière, Le Mèdecin malgré lui

Matthias de L'Obel, after whom the lobelias in our gardens are named, was born at Lille in France in 1538. He studied botany and later moved to London where, in 1570, he and a colleague published a book. They called it *Stirpium Adversaria Nova* and, according to contemporary critics, it was written in extremely bad Latin. However they dedicated it to Queen Elizabeth and from then on L'Obel went from strength to strength, ending up being appointed botanist to the king, *Botanicus Regius*, by King James I. In that book appears for the first time the present common name of one of the most brightly colored of our local wildflowers. "*Lychnis coronaria*," it says, "(anglice) Rose Campion."

Our old friend John Gerard described it most adequately a few years later. "Rose Campion hath round stalkes, very knotty and woolly, and at every knot or joint there do stand two woolly leaves...the floures grow at the top of the stalke of a perfect red colour." He went on to say, "Because the leaves thereof be soft and fit to make weeks for candles, according to the testimony of Dioscorides, it was called Lychnis, that is a torch, or such like light." He then came up with another common name for it, gardener's delight.

Since the Latin word *lychnus* does mean a lamp, Dioscorides, even though he was actually a Greek, got it right. In fact he got so much right in that book of his with the Cratevas' drawings, that his advice and opinions were still being taught and followed 1800 years after he wrote it, when "the medicine which we practise by a completely new method" started to appear. That's a fairly good record.

A copy of this great work, with nearly four hundred full-page drawings of plants, was made in the year 512, to be presented to Princess Juliana Anicia, the daughter of Emperor Flavius. After a long history, during which the book had been, at some stage, in the hands of Harmon, a Jewish physician, who added the Hebrew names of the plants to the

91

drawings, probably while he was employed by Suleiman the Great, it went up for sale in Constantinople in 1562. The Holy Roman Empire's ambassador to the court in Constantinople was an avid book collector and he wrote home to the emperor saying that "the price of a hundred ducats was a sum for the Emperor's purse, not for mine" and that he would have to forgo the pleasure of owning this fabulous volume.

The ambassador must have been fairly persistent, for seven years later, the next emperor, Maximillian, got the message and bought the book, which he placed in the Imperial Library in Vienna. It can still be seen today in the Austrian National Library, the oldest and most valuable book on plants in the world.

But back to the rose campion—rose because of its color, although it looks much more magenta than pink, and campion because it is a champion plant. *Coronaria* means fit for a crown.

Other common names for this striking plant include mullein pink, because its soft leaves, although much smaller, are of the same color and texture as those of the great mullein and lambs' ears, again because of the feel of the leaves, which resemble those of the *Stachys lanata*, to which that particular common name is generally applied.

And, apart from making "weeks for candles," the rose campion has no other uses at all, beyond being a gardener's delight.

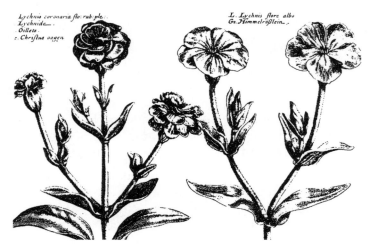

WILD CHRYSANTHEMUMS

Bring corn-flag, tulips and Adonis flower,
Fair oxeye, goldy locks and columbine.

Ben Jonson, Paris' Anniversary

By now, readers of this book will have realized that I'm partial to trivia. Trivia comes from two latin words, *tri* and *via*, meaning three roads, for the Romans used to put up notice boards wherever three roads met and passers by could leave messages there for other travelers. Most of these were of no interest to most people, "Don't forget the milk, Joe," sort of thing, so one could say that they were really quite trivial. And that just leads into another piece of the same, concerning Ben Jonson, who was an English poet and playwright, whose first successful play, *Everyman in his Humour*, had William Shakespeare as a member of the cast. Not too many playwrights can claim that.

So on to the "fair oxeye," which we now call the ox-eye daisy. Its botanic name, *Chrysanthemum leucanthemum*, is rather unfortunate and confusing, for it translates as 'the white-flowered gold flower,' which would be of remarkably little help to anyone trying to identify it from its name alone. Even the common name bears little relationship to the truth. I have never tried to look an ox in the eye, but I'm sure that it wouldn't be white with a yellow center. In fact, the only sensible part of the whole name is the comparison to a daisy, for this favourite tall flower of the road sides and fields in midsummer looks just like a larger version of the little daisies and also, of course, like the well-known garden flower, the Shasta daisy. It is, in fact, one of the four grandparents of the Shasta daisy, which was bred by Luther Burbank.

Our second local chrysanthemum is the feverfew, *Chrysanthemum parthenium*. Its common name is a corruption of the old herbalists word 'febrifuge,' meaning something which drives away fevers. The modern word for this, antipyretic, somehow fails to convey the same sense of human knowledge. Actually, however, folk medicine has made use of the feverfew for quite a variety of remedies, relieving fevers being one of the least of these. Perhaps its best known use these days lies in its ability to reduce the pain of some migraines, the proof of which lay in a series of scientific experiments carried out at the City of London Migraine Clinic.

The most obvious difference in appearance between the feverfew and the ox-eye daisy is that the feverfew's flowers, although of the same color, are far smaller, being only half an inch or so wide, and grow in clusters rather than individually. Its leaves are much paler green, almost with a yellow tinge, but are still deeply indented like those of all the chrysanthemum family. Both plants are immigrants to North America.

Among the nearly 400 plants whose pictures appear in Dioscorides' book is one which he names the 'parthinium', which is this same plant that carries the name today. The word is derived from the Greek for a virgin, as was the Parthenon or Temple of the Virgins in Athens, but exactly why it was applied to this particular plant has long been forgotten. It is probably correct that this should be so, for one of the English herbalists wrote that the plant was "a general strengthener of wombs" and a remedy for "such infirmities as a careless midwife has there caused," matters for which no virgin, ancient Greek or otherwise, should require treatment.

THISTLES

Nemo me impune lacessit.

Scottish Royal Motto

The correct English translation of that would be "no one provokes me with impunity," but the Scots themselves have a more down to earth version, "Wha daur meddle wi' me?" or "Who dares to meddle with me?" for those who don't understand Scots. This unofficial version is, perhaps, a fair reflection of the often prickly nature of the Scot. And what better flower could have been chosen to epitomize this attitude than Scotland's national emblem, the thistle?

Legend has it that the thistle was adopted as the Scottish flower back in the middle of the tenth century, when a member of a Norse war party, creeping ashore barefoot at night near Staines Castle, trod on a thistle. His howls of pain awakened the garrison, who killed or drove off the invaders. In recognition of the thistle's part in this, the King of Scotland declared it to be the national emblem for ever more.

Most thistles are part of a family of plants with the botanic name, *Cirsium*, which comes from the Greek word *kirsos*, meaning a swollen vein, for thistles were used in some way in the treatment of that problem. They are found throughout the whole of the Northern Hemisphere and there are at least 200 different varieties of them, not counting the other plants which look like thistles but are not, such as our local sow thistle.

At least three of the various *Cirsiums* are common in this area. The one most often seen is the *Cirsium arvense*, which actually means a field thistle, but which has acquired the common name of Canada thistle, even though it is not native to Canada. It came here as an uninvited immigrant from Europe and its proliferation is due to the fact that, as well as spreading in the normal way through its seeds, it also sends out underground runners off which new plants sprout and this makes it extremely difficult to eradicate from farm land. In many jurisdictions around the world, there is legislation making it illegal to allow the plant to set seed on one's property.

The second most common family member is the bull thistle, *Circium vulgare*, which is a sturdier and more vicious plants, looking more like the traditional Scottish thistle than the Canadian variety. In addition to having sharper needles along the edges of its leaves, it has another row on the top surface for good measure.

The *Cirsium edule*, or edible thistle, is by far the tallest of these three, and can often grow to eight feet tall, making it fairly obvious to lost travelers, who can eat the lower part of the fleshy stem for sustenance.

According to Gerard's herbal, the soft thistle seeds were used "by the poore to stop pillowes, cushions and beds for want of feathers," but he also complained that rich upholsterers mixed it in with feathers and down, without telling their clients and that "such deceit should be looked into."

Earlier on, it was mentioned that the Linnaean system of classification is used for animals and birds, as well as for plants. The old Roman word for a thistle was *carduus* and, in fact, all thistles were called by that name until the *cirsium* species was separated out. A bird which loves to feed on thistle seeds is the goldfinch and because of its being seen frequently, perched on thistles, it was given the name *carduelis*, meaning belonging to the thistle. Our local bird, the American goldfinch is called the *Carduelis tristis*, or sad thistle bird, and was called that because in the breeding season, the adult male bird wears a black cap on his head as though he were in mourning.

Sometimes it all makes sense, doesn't it?

BLACKBERRIES

And thorns shall come up in her palaces, nettles and brambles in
the fortresses thereof: and it shall be an habitation of dragons and
a court for owls.

Isaiah 54:13

At the time that Isaiah prophesied this great disaster which was to befall
the enemies of Israel, it sounded like a pretty dismal picture, but
perhaps in these days, it doesn't seem quite so bad. After all, knocking
down military establishments and letting blackberry patches grow there
instead isn't such a poor idea. Perhaps having dragons around while one
is out picking berries for a batch of homemade wine might be a bit
disconcerting, but the owls would be fine...they're rather nice birds.

Sometimes the word bramble is applied to the whole of the Rubus
family, which includes blackberries, raspberries, salmonberries and all
of the naturally and artificially hybridized derivatives from these, such
as loganberries and tayberries. But to a Scot, a bramble is a blackberry
and nothing else. Bramble jelly means blackberry jelly, not raspberry
jelly or any other sort of jam.

We have three different varieties of
blackberry growing wild here on the islands and surrounding areas. The most
common of these is the Himalayan
blackberry, *Rubus procerus*, which almost
everybody can recognize. *Rubus* just
means red, because at one stage or another, all of the berries on this family of
plants turns red. The blackberries, of
course, continue on to be a shiny black
color when they're fully ripe. Although
the Himalayan variety is so common
here, it is not native to this area but
arrived with the settlers. It not only
spreads through its seeds being dropped
by the birds which ate the fruit, but it
also roots itself easily, wherever the tips
of its long and bending branches touch

The Bramble Bush

97

the ground. This plant also appears occasionally under a second botanic name, the *Rubus discolor*, the second word meaning two-colored and referring to the fact that the upper surface of the leaf is green, whereas the underneath is silvery.

The evergreen blackberry, *Rubus laciniata*, has much more jagged edged leaves, which stay on the branches all winter, hence the evergreen description. *Laciniata* just means rough edged, and comes originally from the Latin word for the bottom hem of a dress, which, if the dress is ankle-length as the Romans used to wear them, would soon become ragged if one walked around beside the blackberry patch.

Our third local variety is the trailing blackberry, the *Rubus ursinus*. As the name implies, it trails across the ground, rather than standing up like a proper bush. It also scratches ones legs and trips up anyone who tries to walk through the long stems, which are often hidden in the grass. The word *ursinus* comes from the Latin word for a bear, as in the constellation *Ursa Major*, the Great Bear or the Big Dipper as it's often called. Bears like to eat blackberries too.

And just in case anyone dismisses Isaiah's prophesy because it can't happen here, it might be worthwhile noting that the next verse goes on to say, "The wild beasts of the desert shall also meet with the wild beasts of the island."

How do we know which island he was talking about?

PEARLY EVERLASTING

Don't view me with a critic's eye,
But pass my imperfections by.
Large streams from little fountains flow,
Tall oaks from little acorns grow.
David Everett, Lines Written for a School Declamation

I read somewhere that the second most popular street name in North America, next only to Main Street, is Oak Street.

Few of us are naive enough these days to expect that an Oak Street would be a street lined with oak trees. Most of us realize that those who would manipulate our minds in order to lessen the weight of our wallets tend to use names for whatever they're selling that appeal to us in one way or another. That's why Pampers are not called Indulgers and Pert shampoo isn't Saucy shampoo, although these other words are perfectly good alternatives.

Possibly before subdivisions filled B.C.'s Fraser Valley, Cloverdale really was a place where clover grew in a dale. Maybe there did used to be a grove of alder trees at Aldergrove and a long meadow where Langley now stands. Perhaps, before it was blacktopped over for a parking lot, golden flowers grew beside a ford at Guildford, but not necessarily so. The developers knew that those names would attract people and it has worked out exactly as they anticipated.

But we can all be guilty of this sort of prejudice for or against a name. We might call our daughters Rose or Iris, but have you ever met a Geranium or a Larkspur? We might have a son named Basil, but it's not very likely that we'd have one named Parsley and that isn't because those plants whose names we reject are less beautiful, or that they possess some characteristic which we would not wish to be associated with our children. It's pure prejudice and nothing more.

My wife creates dried flower arrangements and sometimes uses stems of pearly everlasting, which is a common wildflower in this area. Its botanic name is *Anaphalis margaritacea*. What *Anaphalis* means is uncertain. A possible explanation is that it comes from the Greek word *knaphalon*, which means a tuft of wool, for the dense clusters of little white flowers which form the head of this plant do look quite like that. But it was the *margaritacea* part of the name which set off this train of

99

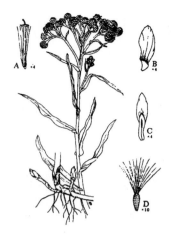

thought. *Margarita* is Latin for a pearl and it was obviously used in the name because everyone could see that the flowers looked pearl-like.

There are lots of women named Margarita, or Marguerite or Margaret. It's a pretty name. A pearl is pretty too, but so for that matter is an emerald and I've never heard of any girl being given the Latin name for that jewel. Sheer, blind prejudice it has to be!

But come to think of it, though, I don't think that I would want to name one of my daughters Smaragdus.

TANSY

Let women that desire children love this herb, for it is their best
companion, their husbands excepted.

Nicholas Culpeper, The English Physitian

Culpeper, who lived from 1616 to 1654, was an English apothecary
and herbalist. He was also a bit of a free spirit, for when he saw that
the poor could not afford the fees which doctors charged to write a
prescription, he made a translation of the *Pharmacopoeia*, the prescription recipe book produced by the College of Physicians, from Latin into
English, and published it, so that everyone could then understand the
recipes and make them up for themselves. This made him so unpopular
with the medical profession that they started a slander campaign
against him, accusing him of being unreliable, inaccurate and down-
right crazy. Even today, that reputation remains attached to his name.

However sympathetic we might feel toward him, though, some of his
treatments, whether they came from the *Pharmacopoeia* or from some
other source, seem slightly odd. As far as tansy was concerned, the
reason why it was a woman's best companion was that, he claimed, it
could be rubbed on the navel of a pregnant woman and prevent her from
suffering a miscarriage.

Both the botanic name of this plant,
Tanacetum vulgare, and the word tansy
itself, which is just a shortened version of the Latin, are derived from the
Greek word *athanasia*, meaning immortality. It has been suggested that
the connection between this common
herb—that's what *vulgare* means,
common—and immortality lies in the
fact that tansy flowers, once they have
been dried, last for ever. But so do the
flowers of many other species of 'ever-
lastings,' so why this particular plant
should have been picked out to have
this one feature especially noted in its
name has never been explained.

The plant is native to Europe and at the time when settlers were coming to North America in the early days, it was considered not only to be an effective medicinal plant, but also a pleasant food flavoring. In addition, oil pressed from the leaves was used as a fly and general insect repellant. Infusions of the leaves were used to treat varicose veins and a tea made from the flowers was thought to be useful in cases of jaundice, perhaps going back to the Doctrine of Signatures and using something bright yellow to treat a yellowing of the skin. In the kitchen, there were tansy-flavored cakes and puddings, particularly during Lent and the Easter season, for this coincides with the Jewish Passover. And Tansy was one of the bitter herbs, according to some, which God had ordered the Jews to eat at that celebration.

Tansy can grow to a height of four to six feet. From stiff stalks thin, dark green, fernlike leaves sprout. The flowers are in loose clusters of small, golden yellow buttons. It grows by the road side where it can draw moisture from the ditches and flowers in July and August.

But a final word of caution, too much tansy can be decidedly fatal. As Culpeper himself put it when he was writing about foxgloves, "the cure can end in the churchyard."

CHICORY

If you wake at midnight, and hear a horse's feet,
Don't go drawing back the blind, or looking in the street.
Them that asks no questions isn't told a lie.
Watch the wall, my darlings while the gentlemen go by.
Rudyard Kipling, A Smuggler's Song

Once upon a time, a beautiful German princess was abandoned by her husband, the prince, whom she loved dearly. Grief stricken by her loss, she was close to death when she whispered to her ladies-in-waiting by her bedside, "I would be happy to die, if only I could see him again, wherever he may be." The ladies-in-waiting echoed their beloved princess wish. "We too would die willingly, if only he could see us watching for him everywhere he went." God heard and took pity on the women. Clothing them all in blue, the color of the princess' eyes, he set them by the road sides to watch for the prince and his gentlemen. Watchers of the road, *Wegewarten*, is still a common German name for the brilliant, blue-flowered plant which we know as blue sailors or chicory.

Chicory is a close relation of the dandelion. They both have the deeply indented leaf edges which gave the dandelion its name and their flowers are of the same size and shape, the only obvious differences being the bright blue color of the chicory and the fact that it grows more like a small bush, unlike the single-stemmed dandelion.

According to most references, chicory is one of a group of plants, whose flowers only open in the morning and then close up from noon onwards until sunrise the next day. If that is so, nobody told our local plants, for they seem to stay awake all day and only close their eyes and turn to the wall at night, when the gentlemen go by.

Chicory has a long history as a food item. To the ancient Egyptians of 5,000 years ago, it was an important salad vegetable. To the Jewish people, it was one of the bitter herbs which God commanded them to eat at Passover. The Romans ate it, the Greeks wrote about it and Charlemagne ordered that it be grown in his garden. The great English herbalists all proclaimed its virtues, calling it 'succory.' Syrop of succory was a popular mild laxative given to children and the milky juice from the stems was recommended as a treatment for kidney problems. John Parkinson, who took over from Matthias de L'Obel as the king's

103

herbalist, wrote that it is "a fine cleansing jovial plant."

Thomas Jefferson, the third president of the United States, was suspected, during his last year in office, of treason, for communicating with the enemy, Great Britain. It turned out that all he was trying to do was to have some chicory seeds sent over to him to plant in his friend, George Washington's garden.

Some of the world's earliest consumer protection legislation was made necessary by the activities of dishonest coffee dealers, who roasted and ground chicory roots and added this in large quantities, without admitting that they had done so, to the coffee which they then sold as 'pure' to the unsuspecting public. One dealer in Liverpool even managed to form the ground chicory into pellets, which he sold as coffee beans at a considerable profit.

In Belgium, chicory growers selected the best strains of the plant, tied the leaves around the stems, mounded them up with earth and blanched them by preventing sunlight from reaching them. What resulted was a vegetable whose leaves had lost much of their bitterness and which is now very popular in Europe, under the name of Belgian endive. In Italy, selective breeding brought about a variety with red-tinged leaves, which they call radiccio, which has become one of the trendy menu items in many North American restaurants.

All this from a dusty little roadside flower.

CHOCOLATE LILY

A lily of a day
Is fairer far in May,
Although it fall and die that night,
It was the plant and flower of light.
In small proportions we just beauties see;
And in short measures, life may perfect be.
> *Ben Jonson, To the Immortal Memory of Sir Lucius Carey*
> *and Sir M. Morison*

On a warm May afternoon, my wife and I were walking along through grassy meadows at the top of the cliffs with a friend named Jerka, who was visiting from Czechoslovakia. After a while, we came across a scattering of flowers, whose mottled brown, bell-shaped blooms swung downwards from eight-inch stems. Jerka stopped and knelt down beside them.

"What do you call these?" he asked. Now we could have given them any of several different common names, chocolate lily, rice root, mission bell and so on, but the name which immediately came to my wife's mind and the one which she spoke out loud was the name which is more often given to one of the cultivated varieties of this plant.

"Fritillary," she replied.

"That's what we call them back home too," Jerka answered, "Fritillaria." And that's the botanic name of our lovely, endangered chocolate lily, the *Fritillaria lanceolata*.

It's always nice to know the reason why a particular plant has been given its special botanic name, partly out of simple curiosity but also because it helps one remember it. In the case of the *Fritillaria*, however, the source of the name is open to some doubt. *Collins Latin English Dictionary* defines a *fritillus* as a dicebox, but since there are no known pictures of a Roman dicebox, one can only try to guess in what way it might have resembled this flower.

In a book printed in France in 1583, it is claimed that a druggist in Orleans, Noel Capperon by name, was the person responsible for coming up with this name. Until then, and to some extent even today in nursery catalogues, this flower or a close relative was called *Flos*

L. Fritillaria flore purpureo

Meleagris, the Flower of Meleager, Prince of Calydon. But perhaps because the pattern of spots on the petals reminded him of something he had seen, Capperon decided that the flower looked like a *fritillus* and called it the 'fritillaria.' Fourteen years later, however, John Gerard had a different explanation. He thought that a *fritillus* was "the table or boord upon which men playe at chesse." From this he concluded that the petal markings were in a checkered pattern and that herein lay the connection. While he was at it, he came up with various other common names such as turkey-hen, ginny (Guinea) hen and chequered daffodil.

So there you are. All I know for sure is that, whenever we see this pretty flower in bloom, we think of Jerka.

MINT

Be not curious in unnecessary matters, for more things are shown unto thee than men understand.

Ecclesiasticus 3:23

Leaf of
Mentha aquatica

Leaf of M. arvensis

Caius Plinius Secundus, a Roman contemporary of Christ and commonly known as Pliny the Elder, was one of the world's first famous naturalists. In total, he wrote thirty-seven books on the subject of nature, covering everything from anthropology to zoology and throwing in a history of fine arts for good measure. Although this earned him an A for effort, most of his material was second hand and from dubious sources, so he has to be awarded a failing grade for accuracy. However, ignoring the advice of Ecclesiasticus, he was insatiably curious and, when Vesuvius erupted in 79 A.D., he just had to go and see for himself what was happening. As the saying goes, it was the death of him.

In his book on botany, Pliny admitted that his favourite plant was mint. "The very smell of it reanimates the spirit," he wrote. Which of the various members of the mint family he was writing about is not very clear. But it might have been what we now call penny royal, *Mentha pulegrium*, for Pliny himself gave it that name from the Latin word *pulex*, meaning a flea, because the scent of the leaves kept fleas away. More probably, however, he was referring to the common wild mint, *Mentha arvensis*, which just means 'field mint,' and which grows throughout the Northern Hemisphere.

The mints are all members of a very large plant family with more than 3,000 species and varieties, including such other well-known garden herbs as thyme, sage, rosemary and lavender. They, the mints that is, appear to cross-pollinate occasionally, giving rise to naturally occurring hybrids, of which peppermint, *Mentha x piperita* is the best known. That 'x' in the botanic name just means that the plant is a crossbreed. Peppermint was first recorded by a Dr. Eales in Hertfordshire, England, in about 1694 and was thought to be a cross between watermint and spearmint.

As a rough and ready guide to identification, common features of the members of the mint family include stems that are square in shape and can easily be felt to be so. Leaves grow in pairs opposite each other and tight against the main stems and their flowers, pale lilac, pink or white in color, grow in tight little balls between where the upper pairs of leaves sprout from the stem. In addition, of course, a slight squeeze of a leaf will release the distinctive mint smell from the menthol oil which it contains.

Spearmint was the only family member which Nicholas Culpeper mentioned in his 1653 herbal. "I have frequently cured and healed many young ladies of weak, delicate, relaxed and consumptive habits of body, by ordering them to go with the maid a milking for a few mornings, and take with them a new laid egg beaten up with a large table spoonful of Rum, and a little Spear Mint cut small, to which add about a tea cup full of new milk from the cow; these being beaten all together in a basin and drunk in the field, with the addition of the morning air, have done wonders."

And as for where the name 'mint' came from, Minthe was a nymph in Greek mythology with whom the god Pluto fell in love. His jealous wife, Persephone, turned the girl into a plant and all that Pluto could do for her was to give her a pleasant scent, to remind those who smelled it of her.

LEMON BALM

Is there no balm in Gilead; is there no physician there?
Why then is not the health of the daughter of my people recovered?
Jeremiah 8:22

It wasn't the Ontario poplar tree, the *Populus candicans*, otherwise known as Balm of Gilead, that Jeremiah was talking about. But it could have been lemon balm.

One reference to lemon balm says that, in 1677, it could be bought at 'William Lucas' shop at the Sign of the Naked Boy, near Strand Bridge in London. The only trouble with that is the inescapable fact that Strand Bridge, designed by the Scottish architect John Rennie, was not started until 1811. It was completed at a cost of £1,050,000 in 1817 and its name was then changed to commemorate the Duke of Wellington's victory two years earlier at Waterloo, and Waterloo Bridge it has remained since then. There was no Strand Bridge in 1677, and unfortunately that throws doubt upon the existence of William Lucas and the Sign of the Naked Boy, which is a pity, for it had the makings of a good story.

However, there is no such doubt about the existence of Caius Secundus Pliny or his thirty-seven natural history books, in one of which he noted that, as far as lemon balm was concerned, "bees love this herb above all others." He even stated that "when bees stray away, they find their way home by it." And still today, as happened 2,000 years ago, there are many beekeepers who rub the entrance to their hives with lemon balm, so that the lemon-mint scent will keep the little insects coming home, rather than straying off anywhere else.

The botanic name for this plant is *Melissa officinalis*. In view of its history, it's hardly surprising that the first of these words should come from the Latin word for honey, *mel*. And whenever the word *officinalis* appears in a botanic name, it signifies that the plant used to have a recognized medicinal application. Over the years, this one has been prescribed for "the stingings of venomous beasts and the bitings of mad dogs," "to heale up greene woundes that are cut with yron,"

and to treat "these that cannot take breathe unlesse they hold their neckes upright." The old apothecaries and herbalists knew what they were talking about to some extent, for lemon balm contains essential oils which have antiseptic and sedative qualities. Because of its reputation, it was brought to North America by settlers and, being a plant which seeds itself very easily, it soon escaped from herb gardens and spread out into the wilds. Although it is still not all that common in this area, it can be found in places with well-drained soil, where it receives full sun.

But there's still one piece of information about lemon balm which perhaps deserves to be tried out. Pliny claimed that it was so strong a medicine for healing cuts that, if it was merely tied onto the weapon which caused the wound, the bleeding would stop by itself. Admittedly, that may be about as accurate as the 1677 Strand Bridge, but there has to be an old army sword around somewhere which we could use for an experiment.

BORAGE

Here, with a loaf of bread beneath the bough,
A flask of wine, a book of verse and Thou
Beside me, singing in the wilderness
And Wilderness is Paradise enow.

Edward Fitzgerald (James Elroy Flecker),
The Rubaiyat of Omar Khayyan

In almost every gardening magazine there is at least one picture of a quiet corner with a cat watching the goings-on of the photographer. Cats and plants have several characteristics in common. In addition to refusing to do what they're told or stay where they've been put, they both sometimes start off wild, allow themselves to be partially domesticated for a while, then revert back to the original wild state again.

One of several local examples of this in the plant world is borage, *Borago officinalis*, which is native to southern Europe, but which was brought here by early settlers as a medicinal herb and planted in their gardens. It found the dry, local climate to its liking and it did not take long for it to escape back into the wild again and establish itself area-wide.

Borage is easy to recognize. It grows to about two feet tall, with heads of bright blue, star-shaped flowers, each with a central white eye surrounding a black cone, formed by the tops of the stamens. No other flower around here has this blue, white and black color combination. The leaves are quite large, coarse looking, grayish green in color and covered with rough hairs. It was these hairs which gave rise to the plant's name.

The Latin word for 'shaggy haired' is *burra*. The Mexican word for a donkey, a *burro*, comes from this too. The Romans called the plant the 'burrago' and in time this changed to the present botanical form, *Borago*, in the same way that the common name changed from the 'burrage' used by writers in the sixteenth and seventeenth centuries to the 'borage' which we have today.

The second word of the botanic name indicates that the plant was once a recognized medicinal herb. The ancient Celtic warriors drank wine flavored with borage flowers to hype them up before battle. The Roman legions, whom the Celts were often fighting, did the same. John Gerard

Borago officinalis

even came up with a scrap of Latin verse, "*Ego borago gaudia semper ago,*" which he said meant "I, borage, always bring courage." Actually, *gaudia* doesn't mean courage. It means joy or happiness, but courage rhymes with burrage, which is more than one can say about joy, so one should perhaps consider Gerard's translation more as a piece of poetic license than a medical prescription. He did at least add, when he started to describe its properties, that it would "drive away sorrow and increase the joy of the mind," if one mixed the flowers in wine.

These days, there is always some research scientist somewhere, usually working on a government grant, who is intent on proving that the John Gerards of this world were wrong. Sure enough, a recent study was done on the effects on laboratory mice of a diet which included borage. The only effect noted was that the mice suffered mild constipation. But how did the researcher try to judge whether the mice were happier or not? And on top of that, there's no mention of wine in the experiment, which one would have thought to be essential. The Romans and Celts thought so.

But if any reader happens to be an unquestioning believer in the power of modern science, there is still a good use for borage in the garden— bees love it. And a few borage plants set in among any vegetable crop needing pollination, such as peas, corn or tomatoes, will attract bees and increase the yield.

On the other hand, many of us agree with Edward Fitzgerald and with the biblical instruction which confirms his views. "Eat thy bread with joy and drink thy wine with a merry heart" and whether a little sprig of borage helps or not, it looks pretty in the glass.

LADY'S SLIPPER

Happy is he who, like Ulysses, has made a great journey...and then came home, full of experience and good sense, to live the rest of his time among his family.

Joachim Du Bellay, Sonnets

Chicken Little was sure that the sky was falling. Everyone else knows, of course, that it can't fall, because Atlas is holding it up. That is his punishment, to hold up the sky on his shoulders forever, for daring to rebel against the Greek gods. And because all of the earliest maps of the world showed him doing so, his name became so associated with maps that an atlas today is called what it is.

Before he got himself into that rather restricting position, or so one must assume, he fathered a daughter, whom he had to hide away from the angry gods. He named her Calypso, which means concealment and sent her to live by herself on the island of Ogygia.

According to Homer, Ulysses, on his way home from the Trojan Wars, became shipwrecked in a storm and was tossed about in the water, lashed to a broken mast, for seven days before he was washed up on the shore of Calypso's island. When they met, they fell in love and he stayed on with her for seven years before getting the itch and deciding that he ought to get on his way again, home to his waiting wife. Calypso offered to make him immortal if he stayed on with her, but he refused her and built a raft with a sail to continue his journey. "The beautiful goddess bathed him first and fitted him out with fragrant clothing. She stowed two skins on his boat, one filled with dark wine and the other, larger, with water, besides a leather sack of corn and other appetizing meats." She then commanded a warm and gentle breeze and sent him on his way. So much for Calypso.

However, she is still remembered more than 2000 years later in the name of one of the most beautiful of our wildflowers, the *Calypso bulbosa*. This is a member of the Orchid family and it is listed as being one of the endangered plants of British Columbia.

As for a common name, there are so many of them for this one simple plant that it would just be confusing to mention them, apart from the one which is most popular in this area, the lady's slipper, which is the

Our Ladies Slipper

name given in Britain to a closely related, yellow-flowered orchid. Bishop George Mountain, the Anglican bishop of Quebec in the middle of the last century, said that this name had come from a rather unsatisfactory translation of an old French common name, *"Le sabot de la Sainte Vierge"* or "The Holy Virgin's wooden shoe." This, he felt, was unsatisfactory because, although "the blossom very closely resembles in form the wooden sabot often worn by peasantry in muddy roads, it has but a disputable resemblance to a slipper, especially that of a lady."

Our own lady's slipper's pink flowers open in May, on stems which are only three or four inches tall and often hidden among the mosses and debris in clearings in the forest. This is how the idea of concealment became associated with the plant and led to its botanic name.

The main reason why the lady's slipper is on an endangered species list is that it can only grow where a particular fungus exists in the soil. Such places are few in number and becoming fewer and fewer as clear cutting of the forests occurs, country roads are widened into highways and where there was once just a forest, there is now a subdivision. In addition to this, people often try to dig them up and transplant them into their gardens, where, because the essential fungus is not present, the plants fold up and die. Even picking the flower in the wild can tear enough of the fragile little roots that the bulb, or tuber if one wants to be absolutely correct, cannot get enough food to survive for the following year. And, as with all wildflowers, picking and carrying away the blossoms also carries off the seeds, which the plant would otherwise have dropped in an area where nature had established the best conditions for germination.

But apart from its rareness and its beauty, perhaps the only thing left to say about this lovely wildflower is to repeat John Gerard's comments, "Touching the faculties of Our Ladies Shoo, we have nothing to write, it being not sufficiently known to the old writers, no nor to the new."

ST. JOHN'S WORT

When Herod's birthday was kept, the daughter of Herodias
danced before them, and pleased Herod. Whereupon he promised
with an oath to give her whatsoever she would ask.
And she, ...said, Give me here John Baptist's head in a charger.
...And he sent and beheaded John in the prison. And his head
was brought in a charger and given to the damsel.

Matthew 14

William Cowper, an eighteenth-century English poet, once described a
plant as being "all blossom, so thick a swarm of flowers, like flies
clothing her slender rods, that scarce a leaf appears." The plant which
he was talking about was St. John's wort, the *Hypericum perforatum*.
Perforatum means the one with the perforated leaves. The devil did that,
with a needle, because he wanted to destroy this plant completely, for
people hung branches of it over their doors and that was guaranteed to
keep him and witches and other unwanted guests out of the house. He
didn't like that at all.

St. John's wort doesn't actually have perforated leaves, it only looks a
bit as though it does. What it has are small transparent glands.

Before Linnaeus came up with the present botanic name, the monks
who drew it in their manuscripts called it *Fuga deamonium*, or devil's
flight, because of its reputations. No one is sure where the name
Hypericum originated, other than it may be a compound of two Greek
words, *hyper* and *icon*, meaning above and image, though what this has
to do with anything is obscure, to say the least.

It became known as St. John's wort for the simple reason that it usually
comes into flower shortly before St. John's day (or Bannockburn Day),
June 24. The fact that, under some conditions, a red-colored juice,
looking rather like blood, can be squeezed from its leaves also helped
the superstitious to connect the plant to the bleeding head of St. John.
And, of course, a plant as steeped in religious significance as this had
to have miraculous medicinal qualities.

John Gerard gave the prescription for "an oile of the colour of bloud,
which is a most pretious remedie for deep woundes and those that are
thorow the body." Nicholas Culpeper claimed that it was "a most noble
anti-venereal." George Herbert, who lived at the same time as these

115

two, wrote that a poultice made from St. John's wort and other herbs had "done great things," although he did not say for what. It has been used as a sedative, a painkiller, an antibiotic and to prevent nausea. Cheese was wrapped in it to prevent spoiling on long journeys, perhaps a result of the antibiotic effect, and it is presently being investigated as a potential organic food preservative for this same reason.

But there are also possible dangers associated with the use of *Hypericum*. Some plants, such as the common herb 'rue,' *Ruta graveolens*, can have the effect of making those who get the oils from the plant on their skin or eat too much of it, highly sensitive to sunlight, so that they suffer from severe burns from only minor exposure to the sun. In Australia, where St. John's wort has become a widespread weed, light-skinned sheep and goats which have grazed on it have been killed by the burns induced through this photosensitivity.

Oscar Wilde wrote a play, based on the character of Salome, Herod's daughter, which was considered so decadent that he could not obtain a license to perform it in England. Twelve years later, Richard Strauss wrote an opera using Wilde's play as the basis. At the first rehearsal, the singer who had been chosen to play the lead, balked at performing the Dance of the Seven Veils, which is merely a strip show with a fancy name. "I won't do it," she is reported as saying, "I'm a decent woman."

ASTER

And there was war in heaven; Michael and his angels
fought against the dragon.

Revelations 12:7

In three of the world's great religions, Michael the Archangel, the
Sword of the Lord, is one of the most important heavenly figures. The
early Christian church made him a saint and assigned a day each year
when a Mass was to be celebrated in his honor.

In the old Roman calendar, originally adopted by Julius Caesar, the
New Year began on March 25, which is why our ninth month, September, was only the seventh month of the Roman year and was named
after the latin word for seven, *septem*. The same goes for the rest of our
year, the months being named after latin eight, nine and ten; *octo*,
novem and *decem*.

Most of the Roman Catholic countries in the world changed to a new
calendar in 1582, on the orders of Pope Gregory XIII. This revised
Gregorian calendar also made other major changes by modifying the
former leap-year system to what we have today and by adjusting the
date, so that the solstices, which by then were ten days out by the Julian
calendar, once more fell on the proper days.

Britain and its American colonies, however, being Protestant countries
by then because of King Henry VIII's falling out with Rome, refused
to change their calendars just because the Pope, whose authority they
no longer recognized, told them to. They continued to use the old
version until the year 1752, by which time it had become eleven days
out of true.

When the change was made in Britain, however, an interesting effect
occurred. George Washington had been born on February 11, 1751,
under the Julian calendar. When the move to the new system happened
in 1752, and New Year's Day was shifted back to January 1st, it had
the effect of making the year of Washington's birth 1752. Then, by
moving the date forward by eleven days, his actual birthday was then
called February 22. So instead of celebrating his birthday on the proper
day, as it was when he was born, it is now celebrated eleven days later.

Amid all of this moving around of dates, the anniversary of the dedication of St. Michael's Basilica in Rome, which was also St. Michael's Day, ended up in the new calendar as being September 29.

In Europe, laborers were paid and rents were payable every three months and the religious holiday which fell nearest to the end of each quarter gained increased significance from this, for it was on those days off work that cash actually changed hands. The end of the third quarter of each year was marked by the Holy Day for the Mass of St. Michael, or 'Michaelmas Day' and as that date approached, people's thoughts naturally turned to how they were going to manage to come up with their next rent payment or how they were going to spend their wages. And as a reminder that the fateful day was coming closer, a tall, daisylike flower came into bloom along the road sides and in their gardens. The star-shaped pattern of the petals of this plant had already resulted in its being named from the Greek word *aster*, which means a star. But to the ordinary country folk, whichever form of this flower grew in their own particular locality became known, as Jean-Jacques Rousseau put it, by "the vulgar title of Michaelmas Daisies."

The most common of the asters which grow in our region comes into flower rather too early, in mid-August, to be truly a Michaelmas daisy. Its botanic name is *Aster subspicatus*, otherwise known as the *Aster douglasii* after David Douglas who first identified it in the Pacific Northwest. It grows to a height of up to three feet, branching widely, with loose clusters of one-inch wide, pale lilac flowers. It prefers to be in moist ground and, since that is also where, in August, other tall plants thrive, the asters are often overlooked among the high grasses.

By the way, in England, when the date was moved forward in 1752, serious riots occurred among those who believed that the date of their future deaths was already known to God and written in his book. They were convinced that eleven days had been stolen off their lives by the dastardly government and they wanted them back again.

Aster

The Scots were far more sanguine about the whole matter. As far as they were concerned, the change merely gave them two New Year's Eves to celebrate, the Old and the New and some of them still celebrate both.

118

NETTLES

Tender handed stroke a nettle
And it stings you for your pains;
Grasp it like a man of mettle
And it soft as silk remains.
Aaron Hill, Verses Written on Window

Perhaps the most useful plant in the world is one which most of us do our best to avoid—the *Urtica dioica* or stinging nettle. Yet this common plant has provided us at various times in our history with clothing, food, medicine, paper, rope, sailcloth, cord for fishing nets and even a high-nitrogen fertilizer for other plants in our gardens.

The earliest known connection between nettles and humans occurred in the form of cloth, woven from nettle fibers, which was used as a shroud and wrapped around a body recovered from a Bronze Age burial site in Denmark. Four thousand years after that cloth was woven, nettles were still being used to make cloth. Thomas Campbell, a Scottish poet who was one of the founders of the University of London in 1820, wrote in a letter, "I have slept in nettle sheets and I have dined off a nettle table cloth...I have heard my mother say that she thought nettle cloth more durable than any other linen."

Even in this century, during the First World War, the Germans are said to have collected nearly 6,000,000 pounds of nettles to spin into thread and weave into cloth when their supply of cotton was cut off by the British naval blockade. In fact, a German word for muslin is *nesseltuch* or nettlecloth, which goes to show that nettles can provide fine material as well as the strong and coarse sails which powered the Viking long ships. As an added attraction, nettles can also be used to dye the cloth woven from them, green from the leaves and stems and yellow from the roots.

As food, nettles again have a long history and in Elizabethan times it was said that a good cook could prepare seven different dishes from this plant. Dishes included plain boiled nettle leaves, which taste like spinach, and a porridge, such as the one which Samuel Pepys served to guests one day in February 1661, noting afterward in his diary that it was very good. Mind you, old Samuel was a fairly generous spirited soul, for only a few days earlier, on January 28, he had written in that

119

same diary that, while at a theater, "a lady spat backward upon me by mistake, not seeing me. But after seeing her to be a very pretty lady, I was not troubled at it at all."

As medicine, nettles were used in a variety of ways, from the Roman treatment of beating paralyzed limbs with fresh nettles to stimulate them into activity, to applying boiled nettle leaves as a poultice, which John Wesley, who was a herbalist as well as a preacher and founder of the Methodist movement, said that he had found to cure a sciatica of forty years standing.

And it wasn't only in Europe that the value of nettles was noticed. All through our area nettles can be found growing close to the sites of Native villages. This fact which was noticed by the first European naturalist to reach here, Archibald Menzies, who traveled with Captain Vancouver in 1792.

As for the botanic name *Urtica dioica*, the first word comes from the Greek *uro* meaning to burn in the way that acid burns or stings the skin. The word 'urine' comes from the same root. *Dioica* means dioiceous, and if that's no help, it means having male and female flowers on separate plants. Holly is another such plant, which is why one has to have both a male and a female holly tree close together before one gets nice red berries for Christmas decorations.

'Nettle' comes from the same Anglo-Saxon word which gave us 'needle,' and that speaks for itself.

YELLOW FLAG IRIS

My heart leaps up when I behold
A rainbow in the sky:
So was it when my life began;
So is it now I am a man;
So be it when I shall grow old,
Or let me die!

William Wordsworth, My Heart Leaps Up

One of the earliest versions of the story of the Creation was written by the Greek poet, Hesiod, in the eighth century B.C. In his epic poem, *Theogeny*, which translates as 'the genealogy of the Gods,' he says that, in the beginning was Chaos. From this evolved Gaea, the Earth Goddess. She then created two husbands for herself: Uranus, the Heavens; and Pontus, the Sea. From unions with these two, the whole panoply of Gods and Titans of Greek mythology came into being. With Pontus, Gaea produced, among many other offspring, a son whom she named Thaumas and he in turn fathered a Goddess who became the messenger to the Gods. Her name was Iris and she appeared to mortals in the form of the rainbow. And from her name and her association with all of the colors of the rainbow's spectrum came both our modern English word 'iridescent' and the name of a whole family of many-colored plants, the Iridaceae or irises, some of whose members can be found in this area.

The yellow flag, *Iris pseudacorus*, is an immigrant from Europe and grows, as Gerard put it, "in moiste medowes, brinkes of rivers, ponds and standing lakes." Although it is not all that common around here, where there tends to be a bit of a shortage of moiste medowes, most people would recognize its tall stem, bright yellow flowers lined with thin purple stripes and its long, pointed leaves as being of the same family as all of those garden varieties of iris, which are so much a feature of springtime.

Another sixteenth-century English herbalist, William Turner, who had to spend most of his life in exile because of his strongly expressed religious views, seems to have got his languages mixed up slightly when he claimed that although the Greeks and the Romans had known the plant as an iris, "it is called in englishe flour de lyce." Be that as it may, it was called in French, *fleur de Louis* after King Louis VII chose it as his badge in about 1140 A.D. Eventually this became the stylized

fleur-de-lis which we know today as the emblems of France and Quebec.

The other member of the iris family which appears around the Georgia Basin is the blue-eyed grass, the *Sisyrinchiums* of various sorts, not all of which have blue flowers. The plants do look very like tufts of tall grass, but from about half way up the blade, a six-petalled flower sprouts, an inch or so wide, usually with a pollen-covered pistil sticking straight out in the middle. A yellow-flowered version, the *Sisyrinchium californicum*, occurs along the coast in Washington and on the shores of lakes and bogs near the sea.

The purple-eyed grass, *Sisyrinchium douglasii*, also called satin-flower, has a larger flower than the others of a royal purple color, although occasionally white, pink or striped flowers are found. Like other of our wildflowers, all of these are matitudinal, which means that the flowers open in the morning and wither by noon. Unfortunately, however, they are so attractive that their flowers are often picked to be carried home for flower arrangements. With the blooms dying by midday, picking them is not only utterly pointless, but the removal of the seeds along with the flowers is rapidly depriving their habitats of new plants to continue the species.

HARVEST BRODIAEA

I sing of brooks, of blossoms, birds, and bowers,
Of April, May, of June, and July flowers.

Robert Herrick, Hesperides

Although Charles Darwin died more than a hundred years ago and many people look upon his words almost with reverence, one of his most basic observations seems to be deliberately ignored. Perhaps that is because it is inconvenient for some to accept the truth in this particular remark, for to do so would be to admit that the human race is in the process of setting off chain reactions which will come back to haunt us and maybe even destroy us.

What Darwin wrote in his *Origin of Species* was, "It is interesting to contemplate an entangled bank, clothed with many plants of many kinds, with birds singing on the bushes, with various insects flitting about, and with worms crawling through the damp earth, and to reflect that these elaborately constructed forms, so different from each other, and dependant upon each other in so complex a manner, have all been produced by laws acting around us."

It has taken unknown millions of years for all of the life forms on earth to evolve and to create their own special places. And one of the simplest ways to see this in action, as far as Darwin's "many plants of many kinds" are concerned, is to watch the growth of wildflowers on our local hillsides over a period of a year.

As the longer days and warmer weather of March arrive, so too do the smallest and lowest growing wildflowers, such as the tiny blue-eyed Mary, which blooms in the short grasses on cliff-side meadows and also the common little roadside daisy.

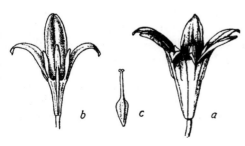

There is good reason why the first flowers to bloom are so low growing. In early spring, the taller plants and grasses have not yet had time to grow up and cut off the light or block the way for pollinating insects to reach these tiny

123

blossoms, so they have to get their flowering period over quickly, their seeds pollinated and the main part of their life cycle finished before it is too late and they are overwhelmed by taller growth around them.

As March passes into April, then May and into summer, taller and taller plants come into bloom in turn, reaching for light and insects above their withering neighbors. Those plants whose seeds are spread by the wind, the thistles and fireweeds, for example, stretch themselves up beyond the shelter of the plants around them so that the wind can strike them and carry their little parachutes far and wide.

In late summer, as the ground dries out and the green growth of spring dies back, shorter plants can once more afford to start their blooming season, taking advantage of the increased light, the lessening of the competition to attract pollinators and the clearer flight path which such insects now have to reach them.

A perfect example of this is the harvest brodiaea, or harvest lily, whose botanic name is *Brodiaea coronaria*. If that seems a difficult name to say, one should try to remember that it is named after James Brodie, a Scottish botanist, and if one can read this sentence out loud, particularly the two words "...Brodie, a..." one has said the plant's name. The flower of this lily does not bloom until late summer or harvest time, after all the surrounding grasses and even its own grasslike leaves have withered and died. Its beautiful violet blossom stands out clearly amid the yellows of the dry stalks around it, acting as a beacon to bees.

In fall, the tall asters, the goldenrods and, on the road verges which have been mowed by the road crews, the short fall dandelions, all flower in their turn. Each plant has depended on something else, a slowly growing neighbor, a grass which dries out when the rains stop, the shade of a tree or the light let through by the immature leaves of another. And this interdependence goes beyond that, to the insects which pollinate, the grazing animals and the birds which spread the seeds in their droppings and even the human scientists, without whose strains of hybridized plants, many of the world's people might starve.

Maybe draining a pond, logging a hillside or black-topping a country lane won't kill off an entire species of plant or animal or insect, but it could set in motion a train of events which could alter our beautiful corner of the earth for ever.

WESTERN SNAKE ROOT

King David and King Solomon
led merry, merry lives,
With many, many lady friends
and many, many wives.
But when old age crept over them,
with many, many qualms,
King Solomon wrote the Proverbs
and King David wrote the Psalms.
James Ball Naylor, David and Solomon

And Psalm 116 says that "Precious in the sight of the Lord is the death of his saints." Be that as it may, some of them died pretty horrible deaths. We've already had St. Cecilia boiling in a tub and now we have St. Lawrence being barbequed on a gridiron.

Lawrence was a deacon in the early Christian church in Rome, whose particular responsibility was the care of the parish widows, children and poor folk. In 258 A.D. the Roman authorities ordered him to hand over to them the treasures of his church. He turned up with a crowd of poor widows and orphans, whom he presented to the local magistrates, saying, "These are the church's treasures."

For his impudence and lack of proper respect for his betters, he was promptly dumped onto a gridiron to roast to death and is credited with asking, part way through his ordeal, if he could be turned over onto his other side, for the one side nearest the flames was quite done.

Herbe de St. Laurent was so named in France because it was thought to contain a substance which would help burns to heal. The Latin verb meaning to heal is *sanare*, from which our English words sanitarium and sanitation are both derived. So too are both the botanic name and one of the common names of the Herbe de St. Laurent, 'sanicula' and 'sanicle.' The other common name,

which is more usual in North America, is snake root.

We have the western snake root growing fairly abundantly around here. The botanic name for it is *Sanicula crassicaulus*, the second word meaning thick stemmed. It is generally found in damp and shady places, such as beside trails in the woods. It has very distinctive, dark green leaves with yellow-green veins running through them and tight heads of small yellow flowers coming into bloom from May onward.

In Native American medicine, an infusion of the roots of the black sanicle, an eastern variety, was given as a treatment for a nervous disease, now known as chorea, but also known by the common name of St. Vitus' dance. And St. Vitus, of course, was another of those early Christian martyrs, who was put to death forty years after Lawrence. In sixteenth-century Germany, it was believed that good health could be ensured for the coming year by dancing in front of his statue on his saint's day, June 15th. Some people's dancing became so manic in appearance, with twitchings and jerkings, that it resembled the involuntary nervous symptoms of chorea. That's where the common name of the disease came from and why St. Vitus is now the patron saint of dancers.

YELLOW BARTSIA

Adam was a gardener and God, who made him, sees
That half a proper gardener's work is done upon his knees.
Rudyard Kipling, The Glory of the Garden

Pope Nicholas V was a gardener too. He probably spent almost as much time on his knees in gardens as he did in front of his High Altar at the Vatican. Unlike many of the early popes, Nicholas was renowned for both his learning and his piety and in keeping with these characteristics, he was a founder of the Vatican Library and also started the rebuilding of the choir of St. Peter's Church in Rome. And on top of all this, he loved flowers.

Before he was elected pope in 1447 and received the papal name of Nicholas, he had been called Tommasso Parentucelli and had managed to combine his loves of God and plants by working his way up to becoming the curator of the Vatican Botanic Garden. And it is because of this that his name has come down to us today as that of a little flower which grows along our local road sides and which goes by the botanic name of *Parentucellia viscosa*. *Viscosa* means sticky. This pretty plant, with pale yellow flowers and grayish green stems and leaves which feel sticky to the touch, comes to us from the Mediterranean area and seems to have made itself quite at home around the Georgia Basin.

But there is one odd thing about it, for it now commemorates two entirely different people. Linnaeus, who started the classification of plants, originally called this one the *Bartsia viscosa*, after his friend Dr. Johann Bartsch of Konigsberg in Sweden. It still appears under that name in a plant encyclopedia published 100 years ago, but at some time since then, Bartsch has been pushed aside and Parentucelli has taken over, except in the common name, where he still remains, the yellow bartsia. Nicholas has undoubtedly gone on to his just rewards, for:

He that is a garden's friend
Groweth calm and wise,
And after death will rise and tend
A plot in Paradise.
Dorothy Frances Gurney

GOLDENROD

But on the hill the golden rod
And the aster in the wood,
In autumn beauty stood.
William C. Bryant, Death of the Flowers

There are more than 100 types of goldenrod, only two or three of which occur naturally outside North America. The one which we see most commonly around here is the *Solidago canadensis*, but even this appears in different forms. Unless for some reason accurate identification is needed, it is probably enough to know that our goldenrods are about three feet high, with strong stems, narrow leaves all along those stems and with thin branches of flower stalks growing at the top, each covered with small golden blossoms. If one sees a flower like that in the fall, it is probably a goldenrod.

The goldenrod was first discovered by Europeans in the North American colonies in Elizabethan times. The Native people used the flowers in a lotion to cure bee stings and to treat minor wounds and the colonists were apparently so impressed with the results that dried flowers were sent back to London for sale by herb women in the various markets. According to John Gerard, the price was "half a crown an ounce," which was a considerable sum in those days. Again, as in North America, the herb was used primarily to treat wounds, for it was found to help tissue to heal cleanly. From this came its botanic name, *Solidago*, which means to make whole or solid, since that is what the treatment achieved.

But people are funny. After the plant had been imported for many years and sold at a high price, a native-English variety of goldenrod was found growing in a wood near Hampstead, north of London. Almost immediately the value of the imported flowers collapsed, as did faith in goldenrod's healing qualities. The point was noted by the Rev. Thomas Fuller, who wrote in 1660, "when golden rod was brought at great expense from foreign countries, it was highly valued; but it was no sooner discovered to be a native plant than it was discarded." There's a bit in the Bible about a prophet not being without honor, save in his own country. Obviously that applies to plants as well.

That was not the end of goldenrod, however for whether it cured

wounds or not, it was certainly a very handsome plant and as such became so highly regarded as a garden specimen that by the time William Cobbett was making his "rural rides" in the 1820s, he was able to write in an article in *The American Gardener* that goldenrod, "which is the torment of the neighboring farmer, has been above all the plants in this world, chosen as the most conspicuous ornament of the front of the King of England's grandest palace." In addition to that, Thomas Edison experimented with making a rubber substitute from the latexlike juice from the stems and, in 1948, an agricultural experimentation station in Texas was recommending the goldenrod as a farm crop, from which an oil could be extracted to use in chewing gum.

And what do we do here with our local goldenrod? Well, not many of us plant it in our gardens, despite the King of England's good example. People haven't changed...they're still funny.

HOREHOUND

Of all the girls that are so smart,
There's none like pretty Sally.
She is the darling of my heart
And she lives in our alley.
Henry Carey, Sally in our Alley

That same poet, of whom most people have never even heard, also wrote a rather better-known piece, which begins "God save our gracious King, Long live our noble King," etc. but that's beside the point.

Until one sad night when she was hit by a vehicle, our house was ruled by a smart and pretty long-haired Maine coon cat named Sally. She was responsible in a way for making me do something which I would otherwise never dream of doing, destroy wildflowers. Well, to be accurate, just one wildflower, the *Marrubium vulgare* or common horehound, which had invaded every corner of our garden.

Horehound is one of those plants whose seeds are covered with tiny barbs, the idea being that these will catch on the coats of passing animals, be pulled off the stems and eventually drop onto the ground elsewhere to germinate. The first two parts of that plan work very well, but when the passing animal happens to be a long-haired cat, the seeds don't drop off as they're meant to, but stay stuck to the fur until the cat jumps on to a bed in the middle of the night and starts to wash herself. At that stage, some of the seeds always manage to work their way between the sheets and that's much more uncomfortable than having a companion who merely eats crackers in bed. So one has the choice of shutting the cat out of the bedroom, combing the seeds out of her coat before she gets a chance to do it herself, or getting rid of the plants altogether by pulling up all of the horehound plants before they can flower and set their seeds. The third of these options was what I tried, unsuccessfully, to do.

The name horehound has nothing whatever to do with dogs. It is a corruption of an old Anglo-Saxon name, 'hare hune.' A hune was a plant whose identity has been long forgotten. Hare was an old version of our present word hoary, meaning white-haired. And this particular hune was hare because the stems and underside of its leaves are covered with small, white hairs.

Marrubium comes from the Hebrew word *marrob*, which means a bitter juice, for this plant does taste bitter and some authorities claim that it was probably another of the bitter plants which God commanded the Israelites to eat at Passover. It would certainly have been known to them at the time of the Exodus from Egypt in about 1400 B.C., when Passover was first ordained. An ancient papyrus scroll, found in Egypt in 1874 by the German Egyptologist, Georg Ebers and now dated to around 1550 B.C., lists what we now call horehound among 800 drugs used in medicine, cooking, cosmetics and the embalming of bodies before they were  wrapped up to become mummies. It is still used today as an ingredient of cough drops and infused as a tea for the treatment of coughs and bronchitis. Those who brew their own beer can use it as a substitute for hops.

Vulgare means common or rude. These adjectives could also have been applied to some of the other names which I used to call horehound in the middle of the night.

FORGET-ME-NOT

When I am dead, my dearest,
Sing no sad songs for me;
Plant thou no roses at my head,
Nor shady cypress tree:
Be the green grass above me
With showers and dewdrops wet;
And if thou wilt, remember,
And if thou wilt, forget.

Christina Rossetti, When I am Dead

Flowers and memories often go together. Peonies make me think of my grandmother, who grew them along one side of her garden in Aberdeen. My wife thinks of her mother whenever she smells the scent of carnations, for that was the scent of the soap which her mother often used. But the flower which is most commonly associated with remembrance is the scarlet poppy, which a Canadian army doctor, John McCrea of Guelph, Ontario, immortalized in a poem which he wrote in 1915, near the great battlefield of Ypres.

In Flanders fields the poppies blow
Between the crosses, row on row,
That mark our place.

Shakespeare connected rosemary with memories, having Ophelia, driven mad by Hamlet's murder of her father, fall into a river with a garland of wildflowers which she had been picking, clasped in her hand. As she floated to her death, she picked out the flowers, one by one. "Here's Rosemary, that's for remembrance."

A third poet and a third flower. Mary Taylor Coleridge wrote,

Some hang above the tombs,
Some weep in empty rooms.
I, when the Iris blooms,
Remember.

But the prize should probably go to an anonymous English lady, who decided to remember every soldier, sailor and airman and every civilian who had anything to do with World War I, by naming individual flowers in her garden after each of them. The list which she produced forms not only a record of their names, but also of the names of regiments

132

long disbanded and largely forgotten. A kalmia, for example, commemorated Lieut. Murphy. Duchess of Connaught's Own Irish Canadian Rangers. A lilac is Lieut. Norman W. Helwig. The Canadian Greys. Sergeant Ronald Cleaver of The Artists' Rifles became a lily of the valley and Commander Gordon Brodie, Royal Navy, a waterlily. In total, more than 500 people were remembered through flowers in her garden, including—since they were our allies in that

Myosotis arvensis Hill.

"war to end all wars"—Japanese officers. Engineer Lieutenant Commander Muneo Yoshinari became the twenty-fourth cherry blossom in her Japanese garden. Then, having done all this, she set about writing and publishing almost 200 pages of rather ponderous poetry about it.

> Having sung of the brilliance and valor and lore
> Of our Army and Navy and Medical Corps,
> We remembered civilians in various ways
> Had deserved of their country some measure of praise.

The one flower whose very name should be associated with memories, the forget-me-not, was used most appropriately to commemorate soldiers and sailors who were missing in action.

Two types of forget-me-not grow wild here, *Myosotis laxa* and *Myosotis discolor*. The first word *Myosotis*, comes from two Greek words, *myos*, which has come down to us in English, almost unaltered as 'mouse' and *otos*, which means an ear and this name was given the plant because the leaves of another variety which is common in Europe, look like mouse ears. *Laxa* means loose, which is why a laxative is so called and the forget-me-not which has that appellation sprawls loosely on the ground, with its distinctive pale blue flowers. Discolor means two colored, for the flowers of this plant can be blue or yellow or sometimes even pink, but they all grow together on the one main stem. Neither of these, unfortunately, have the robustness of the cultivated garden varieties.

> He that outlives this day and comes safe home,
> Will stand a tip-toe when this day is named
> Old men forget, yet all shall be forgot,
> But he'll remember with advantages
> What feats he did that day. Then shall our names...
> Be in their flowing cups, freshly remembered.
> *William Shakespeare, Henry V.*

CLEMATIS

The cuckoo shouts all day at nothing,
In leafy dells alone,
And Travellers Joy beguiles in autumn,
Hearts that have lost their own.

A. E. Housman, Epitaph on an Army of Mercenaries

Our old friend John Gerard gets the credit for giving this plant one of its common names. "This plant is commonly called Viorna," he wrote, "decking and adorning waies and hedges where people travel, and thereupon I have named it the Travellers-Joy." He then went on to take exception to another name for it, which a Dutch botanist had suggested a few years earlier, *Vitis alba*.

Gerard may well have at least twitched in his grave when the botanic name was assigned. The plant is a member of the Clematis family, whose name was derived from the Greek word *klema*, meaning the young shoot of a vine. So "travellers-joy" became *Clematis vitalba*, from those same two words to which Gerard had objected and which just mean white vine.

Because of their popularity as garden specimens, most people call a clematis a clematis, which is usually the name on the tag hung on these plants at the garden shops. Few of us have ever heard the old names which were given it in various parts of England, where it also grows wild, travellers joy, virgin's bower, old man's beard, gypsy bacca, snow in harvest, and many more. Although plants must have one botanic name common to the whole world, it is a pity that so many of the old country names are disappearing, for they added color and often a bit of humor to everyday talk and kept alive the regional variety, without which bland sterility starts to creep in.

In England, there is a gypsy woman named just Beshlie, who travels around in a gypsy caravan with a goldfinch, called Bennet, for company. She paints delightful watercolors of flowers and some of these have been collected into a small book, which she titled, most appropriately, *Travellers Joy*. In the introduction, she gives some of these old names hobble-gobbles, fair maid of France, humpy-scrumples, and the fascinating kitty-come-down-the-lane-jump-up-and-kiss-me. Unfortunately she does not identify them. There is a fair maids of France, also called fair maids of Kent, which is a *Ranunculus aconitifolius*, a white-flowered member of the buttercup family and a Johnny-jump-up, a small, wild viola which may well be what she was referring to and while looking for these names in other books, other old names appeared. How about gardener's garters, angel's fishing-rod, love-lies-bleeding, and queen of the prairie. All of these and more should be preserved for the joy of future generations of gardeners and plant lovers.

There are very few travellers joys growing in this area, for they like a chalky soil, which is not in great supply. When one does see it or its blue-flowered relative, the *Clematis columbiana*, it is generally because ones eye is attracted to the seed head in fall, as the poet mentioned. This is the fluffy ball which gave rise to the old man's beard idea.

And some more old names to end up with none-so-pretty, ragged robin, lords-and-ladies, squinancy-wort, rest-harrow....

PERENNIAL PEA

There was an old person of Dean,
Who dined on one pea and one bean;
For he said, 'More than that,
Would make me too fat.'
That cautious old person of Dean.

Edward Lear, One Hundred Nonsense Pictures and Rhymes

Mr. Lear may have thought that peas and beans were fattening, but if so, he had never read the journal of his contemporary, David Douglas. Douglas had been sent out to this part of the world by the Royal Horticultural Society in London in the 1820s, to collect plants for his employer. After spending a particularly bad night near Cape Foulweather on the Oregon coast, with hurricane force winds, sleet and an unusually high tide, which forced them to move camp twice, they gave up trying to sleep and, long before dawn, set off along the beach for a village lying sixteen miles to the north. When they got there, they found the village deserted and Douglas later wrote in his journal, "We remained here several days, faring scantily on...*Lupinus littoralis* and from continual exposure to the cold and rain and want of proper sustenance, I became greatly reduced."

Lupinus littoralis, the shore lupin; and *Lathyrus littoralis*, the beach pea, together with all of the other lupins and peas, vetches, clovers and brooms which grow around here are part of a large family of about 13,000 plants which are collectively known as *Leguminosae* or pod-bearers. All of them, from the tall acacia trees of Africa down to our local small-flowered lotus, form their seeds inside pods.

Not all of those seeds, however, are as edible as those of the peas and the lupins. The laburnum tree, for example, is quite common around here, having self-seeded from plants brought in to decorate gardens. In spring, it produces a beautiful display of yellow flower clusters, like downward hanging bunches of small yellow pea blossom. These are followed later by green pods, containing highly poisonous little seeds, which have caused the deaths of far too many children, whose parents have failed to adequately warn them of the danger of eating them.

The word 'pea' itself is mildly interesting. It is derived from the Latin word for the same plant, *pisum*. It came into the English language as 'pease,' hence the old nursery rhyme starting "Pease porridge hot, pease porridge cold, pease porridge in the pot, nine days old." After a few centuries, however, somebody thought that any word sounding as though it ended in a S had to be plural, so a new singular form was created—pea. Fortunately this new form of grammar never caught on, or else we would have to press a 'crea' in our pants and blow our 'no' after we 'snee.'

One of the most striking of our local wildflowers is the perennial pea, the wild sweet pea, whose botanic name is *Lathyrus latifolius*. Long stretches of our road sides are covered with its large pink and purple flowers every August. *Latifolius* just means broad-leaved, but *Lathyrus* is one of those words whose origin is somewhat obscure. In Greek, it meant "something exciting." Probably some ancient Athenian spotted this wild pea growing beside the road one day and dragged his friend along to look at it. "What is it?" the friend would have asked. "I've no idea, but it's something exciting, isn't it?" And "something exciting" it has remained to this day.

That may not be such a stupid idea either. The reason why there are many rivers in Europe called the 'Don' is because the advancing Roman soldiers would stop when they reached a river bank and would often ask some local Celtic native who was standing around, "What do you call this?" The Celt would answer in his own language *"Don,"* which was merely the Celtic word for a river, but the Romans would mark it on their maps as the River Don and so they all remain, and it took nearly 2,000 years for anyone to catch on as to how it happened in the first place.

YERBA BUENA

And Babylon, the glory of kingdoms...shall never be inhabited
...neither shall Arabian pitch tent there...but wild beasts
of the desert shall lie there...and satyrs shall dance there.
Isaiah 13

A few years ago, there was a series on PBS television called *Connections*, in which the narrator, James Burke, traced the connections which, for example, had led from the development of the stirrup through to the invention of the atomic bomb. But it's not only in the world of scientific advancement that connections exist; they are part of every aspect of our lives and the ripples spreading outward from a single thought can link together the most seemingly unrelated of ideas.

"Satyrs shall dance in Babylon." Actually that's rather a peculiar remark for a Hebrew prophet to make or for those learned translators of the King James version of the Bible to incorporate into their final text. For satyrs were the product of paganism, of Greek mythology, in which these creatures, half man-half goat, reveled in lewd and drunken behavior with the nymphs of the meadows and woods. Creatures whose very existence was totally denied by both the Jewish and the Christian religions.

Aphrodite, the Greek Goddess of love, was herself the lover of many other gods, including Dionysus, the God of fertility and wine, which one might consider to be a fair enough connection right there. She has given her name to love potions—aphrodisiacs—and throughout the whole history of mankind, there have been men who sought the perfect one. In Africa, men grind up rhinoceros horns and sprinkle the powder on their food. Chinese believe in the power of bird's nest soup and bear paws and in western countries, every possible plant has been tried out in the hope that one of them might prove successful. One plant whose reputation for effectiveness in this line eventually caught on, was a small member of the mint family and somebody, probably the Roman equivalent of a snake oil salesman, thought that it would be a good idea to give the plant a name which would connect it in people's minds to the creatures which followed Dionysus, the satyrs. So *Satureja* it became and men wolfed it down, hoping that it would give them the prowess of billy goats.

138

The actual plant which was used in this way in Europe is the one which is now known as summer savory, *Satureja hortensis*, and which is often found in herb gardens to be used, in these more enlightened days, as a flavoring. It is frequently cooked with beans, since it is thought to have antiflatulence qualities. It does not grow wild here, but a close relative does, *Satureja douglasii*, named after David Douglas, who came across it in the Pacific Northwest. In fact, the Spanish explorers who were here first had also found it and, because of its pleasant taste, had named it "the good herb"—*yerba buena*, and that remains its common name.

It is a low, ground-hugging trailer, with stems of up to a yard in length, with pairs of savory leaves opposite each other and pairs of white or pale lavender, tubular flowers. Its value as an aphrodisiac, however, would be about as great as one's hopes of finding a satyr in Babylon.

PINEAPPLE WEED

Who ran to help me when I fell,
And would some pretty story tell,
Or kiss the place to make it well?
My Mother.

Ann Taylor, My Mother

And her daughter wrote "Twinkle, twinkle, little star," another piece of trivia.

If you find yourself standing by the road side in a dry, open area, on a sunny summer day and look down near your feet, the chances are that you'll see a small plant there, with very finely divided leaves and a dull yellow flower, which looks like a daisy with all of its petals pulled off. If it's there, bend down, squeeze one of the flowers and smell it. Then you'll know where its common name, the pineapple weed originated.

This pleasant little herb has one of botany's silliest botanic names, the *Matricaria matricarioides*. This comes from two Latin words, *mater*, meaning mother and *cara*, meaning dear. The 'oides' ending means that it is like whatever comes in front of that ending, so in this case we end up with a plant whose name can be translated as 'mother-dear-like mother dear.' It probably started off because of some forgotten association with Mary, the mother of Jesus, whose name was often invoked by people in distress, calling upon "dear mother" to aid them. Sailors in peril frequently used this invocation. If, in the midst of a gale, one particular seabird, the storm petrel, appeared and flew near their ship, the sailors then believed that they would come through the storm safely and that "dear mother," or *madre cara* as the Spanish called her, had sent the bird to them as a sign. From this belief arose the common name of the storm petrel, mother Cary's chicken. More trivia.

Other members of the *Matricaria* family also grow locally. One is the *Matricaria maritima*, which, as its name implies, is a seaside plant. It is very like a larger version of the pineapple weed, perhaps up to a foot tall, but it has the white, daisylike petals which its cousin lacks. It flowers in May and has no scent whatever, which is why its common name is the scentless Mayweed.

A third family member appears occasionally as an escapee from a herb garden. This is the *Matricaria recutita*, the German chamomile. There

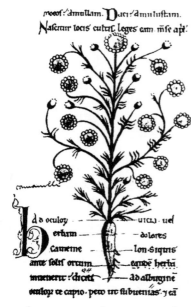

moeof: amullam. Daci: amulustam.
Nafcunr locis cultat leges eam mfe api.

d o oculoz
erbum
camerne
ame folif orcum
muenerit: dictt
eculoz ce capio. pero tuc fubuentas. y ea

utici. uel
dolores
lon sigms
eque herba
ad albugine

is also a Roman chamomile, which has gone through various botanic names and is now usually referred to in botany as the *Chamaemelum nobile*. Each of these two chamomiles has its own supporters, who claim that only their own special favorite is the true herb and that the other is a useless weed. Whichever one might be 'true' however, both are used today as rinses for blonde hair, ingredients of herbal cosmetics and as a tonic in herbal medicine. Both have been grown commercially for these purposes and in nineteenth-century England, school children were given holidays at harvest time so that they could help with the picking of the flowers. Roman chamomile was also used as a ground cover, much as we use grass today, and it gives off a pleasant apple scent when it is walked on. That's where the name chamomile itself came from, the Greek word for a ground-apple.

There was an old saying about chamomile, "The more it is trodden, the more it will spread." The same applies to the pineapple weed, which has spread along our road sides, like the plantain, because of people treading on it, carrying the seeds on the soles of their shoes and treading them into the ground on the next pace.

So there's something to occupy your mind while you're standing by the road in summer.

DAISIES AND BUTTERCUPS

Of all the floures in the mede,
Thanne love I most these floures white and rede,
Such as men callen daysyes.
Geoffrey Chaucer, The Legend of Good Women

If there is one flower around here whose name everyone knows, it has to be the common little white daisy. It was probably the first flower which most of us were ever aware of and whose name our mothers taught us, sitting on the grass and making daisy-chains. Yet these days, inconceivable as it might seem to those who love to see this pretty little plant in bloom, there are others who seem to hate it so much that they squirt chemicals onto their immaculate front lawns to kill it. I'm not at all sure who these people are impressing, for those like themselves who hate daisies are probably far too busy driving around in expensive cars to even notice whether anyone else is allowing them to live or not.

The botanic name for this plant is *Bellis perennis*, which just means a pretty plant which grows year after year, and that about sums it up. The name daisy is a corruption of day's eye, as Chaucer nearly spelled it, and comes from the flower's habit of closing its white petals over the yellow center at night and opening them again, like opening one's eyes, in the morning.

Rather surprisingly for such a well-known plant, no legends seem to have evolved around the daisy, nor was it ever considered to be of much use in herbal medicine, other than in a poultice of its crushed leaves which was sometimes used to reduce bruising. From this arose another, not very common name, bruisewort. John Gerard, however, did suggest a veterinary use for it. "The juice of the leaves and roots," he claimed, "given to little dogs with milke, keepeth them from growing great."

The other spring flower which often seems to go together with the daisy is the buttercup, and it doesn't appear in legends either. Although the buttercup family is thought by botanists to be one of the oldest in the whole plant kingdom, its common English name is one of the newest. Until about a couple of hundred years ago, it was generally called the goldcuppes or the butterflower, but then a merger of these two gave us what we have today. Its association with butter came about through the fact that it likes to grow in lush green meadows where cows were allowed to graze in the spring after having been shut in their cow sheds or farm yards all winter, feeding on hay. Since the color of the cream changed from white to yellow at around the time that the cattle were let loose, actually because nature was increasing the fat content of the milk in preparation for

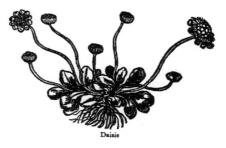

Daisie

feeding the new season's calves, the country folk attributed the color change to the flowers which their cows were eating. They never seemed to notice that cattle try to avoid eating buttercups, since they are mildly toxic to them.

The most common of the several members of the buttercup family which grow here is the western buttercup, the *Ranunculus occidentalis*. The second word means western and *Ranunculus* can be translated as "the smallest frog," presumably because buttercups and their relatives like to grow in marshy ground, near or even in slowly running water, the same sort of place where frogs lay their spawn.

Perhaps it was this connection with water which gave W. S. Gilbert the idea for the name of his Portsmouth bumboat-woman in H.M.S. *Pinafore*, "the rosiest, the roundest and the reddest beauty in all Spithead":

> For I'm called Little Buttercup, dear Little Buttercup,
> Though I could never tell why...

Well, it's no worse than Daisy "looking sweet upon the seat of a bicycle made for two."

TIGER LILY

Consider the lilies of the field, how they grow; they
toil not, neither do they spin: And yet I say unto you
That even Solomon in all his glory was not arrayed like
one of these.

Matthew 6:28, 29

L. *Marragon Pomponeum.*

There is a certain type of person,
whom one might call an 'ologist.'
This is a sort of generic term for a
small group of people who, having
obtained a degree in some subject,
consider themselves to be so far
above the common herd in their
knowledge of whatever it was that
they studied, that everyone else is
utterly ignorant. Somehow these
people often seem to get themselves
government grants to prepare the-
ses on matters which are extremely
obvious to those whom they de-
spise, such as the fact that women
spend longer on average in public
washrooms than men do. And it is my personal belief that whomever it
was who came up with the theory that the "lilies of the field" referred
to in the Gospel were not lilies at all, but anenomes, was probably an
'ologist' too. After all, where did Jesus get a botany degree?

Whether all of this is right or wrong, one plant which is absolutely
certainly a lily, is equally certainly clothed more gloriously than even
Solomon. This is our native local wild tiger lily, the Columbia lily or
Lilium columbianum. Its territory spreads from southern British Columbia to northern California, from sea level on the islands to 5,000 feet
or more on the Olympic Peninsula. It blooms in June and July, flowering on stems from two to five feet in height, with as many as thirty
blossoms to a single plant, although four or five are far more common.

Unfortunately, because it likes moist ground for its roots, this beautiful
plant often grows near ditches beside our roads, where it is easily

noticed by passersby. Often one sees people on the islands heading toward a ferry terminal at the end of a day's visit, carrying a bunch of wild tiger lilies, which will have died before they reach home and whose seeds are lost to the island forever. Stopping this loss of an already endangered species is only a matter of education, but how does one go about it?

There is a legend in Korea which tells how a hermit found a tiger, wounded in the leg by an arrow. He healed the wound and the tiger became his constant companion. Years later, as the tiger was dying of old age, he asked his friend to keep his body near him. The hermit changed the beast into a tiger lily and when the hermit himself died, the lily spread to every corner of the land, looking for the old man. How could one pick a flower with a story like that?

SERVICEBERRY

Some have meat, but cannot eat,
Some would eat, but want it.
But we have meat and we can eat,
So let the Lord be thankit.

Robert Burns, The Selkirk Grace

The Earl of Southesk, who traveled off the beaten track in western Canada in 1859-60, had meat. The Indian guides who accompanied him brought pemmican with them, but the Earl was not very impressed by it. "Take scrapings from the driest outside corner of a very stale piece of cold roast beef," he wrote later, "add to it lumps of tallowy rancid fat, then garnish with long human hair (on which you string pieces like beads up a necklace) and you have a fair imitation of common pemmican."

The Native peoples of what are now the prairie provinces sometimes tried to improve the flavor of their pemmican by adding crushed, dried fruit to the recipe and whenever they could get it, the fruit which they most often chose was one which they called '*Meesaskootoom mima*,' or a word like that, depending on whose spelling one is looking at. The French voyageurs called this fruit *petites poires* or little pears, since that is what it resembles, and the English traders had several other names for it, including shadbush, serviceberry, pigeon berry and Indian pear. Eventually, however, the Cree word, slightly shortened, joined the list of names, both for the fruit and for a place where it grew in great abundance—Saskatoon.

The shrub which produces these fruits also grows in this area, where most people are quite happy to leave the fruit to the birds and just enjoy the beauty of the pure white flowers in springtime. It was these white blossoms, coupled with the original Roman name for a closely related European variety of the plant, which gave rise to the common name which appears in nursery catalogues in England, the snowy mespilus. But it

was another local name, the one which was used in the Savoy region of France, *amelancier*, which formed the basis of the botanic name, *Amelanchier alnifolia*. The second word means that the leaves are like those of the alder tree.

And having come up with all of these various names, there's still one more, 'medlar.' This is another close relative of the serviceberry but it never became very popular as a fruit, because its berries are about the same size as peas and, since it grows in places where apples and pears are plentiful, who would want to go to the bother of picking all those small things?

Furthermore, the medlar's fruit is so hard that it has to be left until it is half rotten before it becomes ripe enough to eat. Shakespeare knew about this, for he had one of his characters in *As You Like It* say, "You'll be rotten ere you be half ripe and that's the right virtue of the Medlar."

Although such half-rotten fruit might seem to be an appropriate addition to pemmican, no one has suggested that serviceberries were allowed to reach that state before being added to the mixture. In fact, even the Earl of Southesk had to admit, rather grudgingly, that putting serviceberries into the mix did help a bit. "Carefully made pemmican," he wrote, "such as that flavoured with the Saskootoom berries...is nearly good, but, in two senses, a little of it goes a long way."

OREGON GRAPE

Said the King to the Colonel,
"The complaints are eternal
That you Irish give more trouble than any other Corps."
Said the Colonel to the King,
"This complaint is no new thing,
For your foemen, Sire, have made it a hundred times before."
Sir Arthur Conan Doyle, The Irish Colonel

When the Romans invaded Britain 2,000 years ago, they failed miserably to conquer Scotland and didn't even try to take on the Irish. Possibly as a result of this, a strong prejudice seems to have arisen on the part of those who use the Latin language to give botanic names to plants, for nowhere in the plant lists can one find a species named after anyone with a Highland or Irish name starting with 'Mac.' One can search in vain for a Macphersonia or a MacCarthia, for the Macs have been totally discriminated against.

A prime example of this relates to a particular plant, which someone decided to name after an Irish American botanist, Bernard M'Mahon. In order to comply with the anti-Gaelic rule, the prefix had to be dropped before the name was acceptable, leaving the remainder to be Latinized as merely *mahonia*. To complicate the issue slightly, as far as anyone knows, this plant has nothing whatever to do with Mr. M'Mahon. It was actually identified by David Douglas, who was collecting plants in this general area and shipping them back to the Royal Horticultural Society in London. When he sent the Mahonia back, it was so well received that, for several years, individual plants were selling in England for ten pounds each, a sum which would have had an equivalent purchasing power of about 2,000 of today's dollars.

But the story of the name doesn't end there. When the royal society's experts saw the plant, they decided that it belonged to a family already known as Berberis, or barberry, a name derived from the Berbers of

North Africa. They had got that name from the Romans because they were considered to be barbarous, so calling Mr. M'Mahon's plant after barbarians might well be just another slight on the poor Irish.

To distinguish this plant from its relatives, the second part of the name, *aquifolia*, meaning water on the leaves, was added, because the leaves do appear shiny and wet. So we end up with the *Berberis aquifolia*, the *mahonia*, otherwise known as the Oregon grape, a wild plant common to the Pacific Northwest. It is an evergreen shrub, generally growing to a height of two or three feet. Its leaves are very similar to those of holly, but the older leaves turn bright scarlet, which adds greatly to the beauty of the plant. Bright yellow clusters of small flowers in the spring are followed in late summer by dark purple berries, very like small grapes, which formed part of the diet of the Native people.

As a footnote, David Douglas came to a sticky end, when he went on from here to the Hawaiian Islands to continue his plant collecting. A wild bull, possibly objecting to the removal of native species from their proper habitat, gored him to death. There may be a moral in that.

HAREBELLS

O, dutiful would I Plough my lands,
But not for the pomp that money brings:
I would leave the glitter of sinking sands
For the fragrant quiet where the blue-bell rings.
Andrew Dodds, O, To be Out

In many parts of Europe, just to mention the word bluebell seems to bring back to people memories of childhood, walking through bluebell woods and picking bunches of flowers to carry home. I was reading a book recently, which had belonged to my great-grandmother. It is a description of the New Forest in southern England, month by month throughout the year, with its trees and flowers, birds and animals, each in their season. "The bluebells," wrote the author in May, "are in full beauty and spread a sheet of pure colour across the lower part of the wood near the Two Oaks gate. Oh, to keep them there, just as they are now, for a little longer."

It was nostalgia for sights such as this which caused so many of the immigrants to North America to send back to their old homes for bluebell bulbs. To this day, an old track which used to lead to one of the original farmhouses near my own home can still be traced in spring by the bluebells growing where the farmer's wife planted them beside the ruts.

These flowers, though, which the English call bluebells, are really a form of hyacinth and belong to the lily family. They are not native to this part of the world. What we do have are various members of the group of plants which the Scots call bluebells and write poetry about and also sing songs about, such as "The Bluebells of Scotland" and "Mary, my Scots Bluebell." In England, these are known as 'harebells,' although that ought to be spelled 'hairbell,' since they got their name by having the flowers hang downwards at the end of hairlike stems. The botanic name for a harebell is *Campanula rotundifolia*, which just means the little bell with the round leaves. It is most commonly seen at the higher elevations in our region, as is the very beautiful piper's harebell of the Olympic Mountains. At lower levels, Scouler's harebell is what we have. Its botanic name is *Campanula scouleri* and it was named after Dr. John Scouler, who was a companion of David Douglas on his plant finding expeditions to the West Coast.

This delicate little flower grows to a height of only three to four inches, with a pale blue blossom, from the center of which an extra-long pistil protrudes, making the plant easy to recognize. It is generally to be found in lightly treed areas, where there is a mix of sun and shade, growing alongside mosses and twinflowers.

Going back to the English bluebell for a moment, it has a couple of interesting uses. According to John Gerard, "The roote is bulbous, full of a slimie glewish juice, which will serve to set feathers on arrows in stead of glew."

And Dioscorides, the Roman army doctor who has been mentioned before, wrote in his famous medical text that bluebell roots, beaten and applied with white wine, would "hinder or keep back the growth of hairs."

> Fain would I kiss my Julia's dainty leg,
> Which is as white and hairless as an egg.
> *Robert Herrick, On Julia's Legs*

SALAL

April 9. In the afternoon in company with Mr. Douglas I made a short visit to the shore. The first we collected on North American continent was the charming Gaultheria shallon, in excellent conditions.

Dr. John Scouler, Journal, 1825

Linnaeus, who gave himself the monumental task of classifying all of the world's plants, had a pupil and friend named Peter Kalm. In 1748, Kalm was sent to North America by the Swedish Academy of Sciences to collect plants as part of this great undertaking. One of the people whom he was told to contact for help once he reached America, was Jean-Francois Gaultier, physician to the Quebec seminary and also a corresponding member of the French Academie Royale des Sciences. Gaultier had already been collecting plants and shipping them back to Paris, so he turned out to be one of Kalm's most useful contacts. Together they went out on at least two successful expeditions and in appreciation for this, Kalm named a species of plants after him, *Gaultheria*. A member of this family, the *Gaultheria shallon*, otherwise known by its Indian name of *salal*, is among our most common native plants.

Surely everyone knows salal. Our local woods are full of it, making it almost impossible to wander off established trails. It averages around four to six feet in height, although in the rain forests of the western coast of Vancouver Island it can reach three times that figure. The branches become so intertwined as to be virtually impenetrable. The leathery, dark evergreen leaves, three to four inches in size, are unmis-

takable for those of any other local plant. In May, bunches of small, pink flowers appear near the ends of the stems, similar to but larger than heather bells, for this plant is also a member of the huge heather family. By fall, the deep purple berries which follow the flowers are ripe, and the coastal people used to mash these into a pulp and dry this in slabs for winter nourishment.

Douglas sent seeds of salal back to England and, after they had germinated and grown, the resulting plants created a minor sensation. Foliage is still gathered today and used by florists because of its striking beauty and long-lasting quality.

But it would have been the eastern variety, *Gaultheria procumbens*, which Kalm was shown. *Procumbens* means that it stretches out along the ground as opposed to our own upright variety. The eastern plant became a highly valuable source of oil of wintergreen, which was considered to be of great medicinal value in the treatment of a number of ills from ulcers and toothache to strained muscles. These days the oil is produced synthetically for chewing gums and toothpastes and as an ingredient in liniments.

Incidentally, in November, 1742, Dr. Gaultier set up the first ever meteorological station in Canada, to measure and record the weather, starting a tradition of weather observation which is still continued on behalf of the Federal Government's Environment Service by nearly 3,000 volunteers across the country, including my wife.

PIPSISSEWA

Thro' the rare red heather, we danced together,
(O Love, my Willie) and smelt for flowers.
I must mention again it was gorgeous weather,
Rhymes are so scarce in this world of ours.
Charles S. Calverly, Lovers and a Reflection

Mr. Calverley wrote that about 130 years ago. He was an English barrister, who was so seriously injured in a skating accident that he took time off from the law and started to produce poetry. One hopes that he was a better lawyer than a poet and the only reason he is quoted here is because rhymes about heather are even scarcer than rhymes themselves.

If one goes into any garden center and takes a look at the little labels in pots of heather, the chances are that some of them will read *Erica carnea*, followed by a name such as Springwood White, which happens to be a popular cultivar. And what this is leading up to is that *Erica* is the Latin word for a type of heather.

The Erica family, known as Ericacea, contains a bit less than 2,000 different species of plants, and although we have none of what are usually thought of as heathers growing at our lower elevations, there are several other family members here.

Perhaps the most surprising of these is the arbutus or madrona tree, which is also by far the largest. It mightn't look very much like heather, but if one takes a look at the cream-colored flowers which fall on our roads in millions each spring, they look exactly like heather bells.

Further down the size scale are the native rhododendrons, and try to find a rhyme for that! Both the red *Rhododendron macrophyllum*, whose flowers are actually pink, and the white *Rhododendron albiflorum*, whose tangled branches have caused it to be known as mountain misery by hikers, appear around the Georgia Basin from about the 2,000 foot level, although individual specimens turn up sometimes closer to the water.

Next we have the manzanita, which is the Spanish for a little apple, because that is what the small fruits look like. Its botanic name is *Arctostaphylos columbiana*, which one could translate as "bunches of grapes for bears in Columbia," if one was so inclined. Salal and huckleberry follow, still all part of the same family and with the same bell-shaped flowers until finally one comes to one of the smallest cousins, the *Chimaphila umbellata*, which means something like "the winter-loving plant with bunches of small flowers originating from a single stem." If that's too complicated, one can try one's luck at pronouncing its Indian name, *Pipsissewa*, or just stick with its easier name, prince's pine, which probably came from someone who gave up on the Cree word, for which there is no rhyme either.

Finally, back to the manzanita's little apples. They start off green, but,

> Streaks of red are mingled there,
> Such as are on a Catherine pear,
> (The side that's next the sun)

That was written in about 1640 by Sir John Suckling, who is credited with being the inventor of cribbage. I just had to get that in somehow.

ERYTHRONIUMS

The lily is an herbe with a whyte floure and wythin
shineth the lykeness of golde.
John of Trevisa, De Proprietatibus Rerum

And for those who have never heard of that gentleman, he was born in
Cornwall in 1326, expelled from Oxford University for "unworthiness"
and ended up as Vicar of Berkeley, possibly making one of the first
translations of the Bible into English.

One of the first holidays which my wife and I had, after we came to live
in the Pacific Northwest, took the form of a backpacking expedition
into the higher reaches of the Olympic National Park. Before setting
off, we stopped at Park Headquarters near Port Angeles to get maps and
spotted a small book about the park's wildflowers. What made it stand
out was the cover photograph of an alpine meadow, covered almost to
the horizon with a carpet of white flowers. That was our first introduction to the avalanche lily, the *Erythronium montanum*, which, with its
three close relatives which also grow in this area have to be among the
most beautiful of all flowers, anywhere in the world.

Erythronium comes from two Greek words and means a red flower which
is what the major European variety is. The avalanche lily, however, is
exactly as John of Trevisa described it. It has pure white petals, which
turn to gold as they near the center of the flower.

Over the next few years, we continued to hike the high back country of
the park each summer, but although we found ourselves in many
incredibly beautiful alpine meadows, we never found the one where the
anonymous photographer from the Olympic Natural History Association took that glorious shot. We did, however, find a second member of
the *Erythronium* family, which also grows in the park and on many of
the mountains surrounding the Georgia Basin. This is the glacier lily,
the *Erythronium grandiflorum*, a yellow-flowered version of the white
avalanche lily. Both of these usually have two, but occasionally three,
bright shiny green leaves growing at the base of the flower stem.

Closer to sea level grow two other *Erythroniums*, this time with leaves
spotted with brownish dots, which gave rise to two of the plants'
common names. The first plant is the *Erythronium oregonum*, also

known as the white fawn lily, Easter lily, trout lily, Oregon lily (from its botanic name), adder's tongue and dog tooth violet, and probably by other names as well. The fawn and trout connections obviously lie in the spots on the leaves. It flowers in April, which can be at the same time as Easter, and its pistil may look something like an adder's forked tongue. Its bulb, which provided food for our Native peoples, is white and shaped rather like a dog's tooth, but it is certainly not a violet, so where that name came from is anybody's guess.

The last of the local relations is the pink fawn lily, the *Erythronium revolutum*, which is virtually identical to the white version except, of course, for the color of its petals. Which of the two fawn lilies one finds seems to depend to a large extent upon the type of soil in the particular area. The pink flowers grow where the soil is sandy and the white ones where there is more organic matter in the ground. On Vancouver Island, near Honeymoon Bay beside Lake Cowichan, there is a magnifi-
cent small wildflower reserve which was established by a forestry company. In late April and early May, visitors can see masses of these pink fawn lilies growing by the river along with trilliums, wild ginger and a host of other flowers and trees.

Ben Jonson wrote,

> Have you seen but a bright lily grow,
> Before rude hands have touched it?

For those who have, it is a sight never to be forgotten.

FLOWERING RED CURRANT

And now abideth Faith, Hope and Charity, these three;
but the greatest of these is Charity.

1 Corinthians, 13:13

The Corinthians to whom St. Paul wrote these words were a small group of Christian converts, living in the city of Corinth in Greece. Corinth was already 800 years old or more when Paul visited it and it had become one of the largest, wealthiest and most powerful cities in the world. But rapid growth in a city often brings with it serious social problems, not just in the twentieth century but back then too. Crime and licentiousness abounded in Corinth, encouraged perhaps by the practices of idolatry and the worship of all sorts of strange gods in this most cosmopolitan of ancient cities. The Roman poet, Horace, who died in the year 8 B.C., and who seems to have enjoyed the bright lights to some extent, wrote, "Not everyone is lucky enough to get to Corinth," which gives some idea of what was going on there and why Paul felt compelled to write two letters to his friends, encouraging them to stay on the straight and narrow path.

Part of the wealth of the city, and perhaps of some of the city's Christian community too, was derived from the export of raisins, the dried fruit of certain varieties of grapes. One such variety was, and still is, the zante or black Corinth, which is also grown these days in California. The raisins produced from these grapes were exceptional for their firm texture and sharp flavor and Corinth raisins became famous throughout Europe. Eventually the name was shortened into just 'Corinths' and by Elizabethan times it had been corrupted in common speech into what we say today, 'currants.'

But to confuse the issue slightly, the plants which we now refer to as currant bushes and the red, white and black currants which they produce, are of a totally different species from the black Corinth grapes. Grapes belong to the botanic family called Vitis, meaning a vine. Currant bushes and their fruits belong to the Ribes family, which also includes gooseberries, and are native to North America, from whence they were introduced into Europe by returning travelers in the sixteenth century. At first they were called beyond-sea gooseberries and then bastard currants, which annoyed several contemporary herbalists,

158

including John Gerard, who pointed out that these new fruits were definitely not currants and shouldn't be called that. However the name stuck and the popularity of the little berries grew and now the word can mean either the fresh fruit of the Ribes or the dried fruit of the Vitis.

In 1827, David Douglas came across the flowering red currant growing wild on the banks of the Columbia River. He sent some of its seeds back to the Royal Horticultural Society and the plants which these seeds produced, with their almost fluorescent pink flowers, were so strikingly beautiful that there was an instant demand for them from gardeners. So great was the demand, in fact, that the entire cost of Douglas' two-year expedition was quickly paid off from the sale of this one plant.

The flowering red currant is one of the earliest of our native plants to show color in the spring, coming into bloom in early March, before even its own leaves appear, and it keeps on blooming through into May. One just has to see it or its white-flowered version to realize why it made such a hit in London and Paris a century and a half ago.

The plant's botanic name is *Ribes sanguineum*. *Sanguineum* means bloody, and relates, of course, to the blood red color of some of the darker pink flowers which are sometimes found. *Ribes* comes from ribas, a medical name which the Moors gave to a totally different plant which grows in North Africa and Spain, so one can say that insofar as both the botanic and common names of the currant are concerned, somebody sure got it wrong.

THIMBLE BERRY

On the rocky islands and in the woods...is a species of
raspberry of the most delicious flavor, and far superior to
any fruit of that kind we had ever before tasted.
*John Meares, Voyages made in the Years 1788 and 1799
from China to the N.W. Coast of America*

Clayoquot Sound is a name which has become quite familiar around
the world as an area on the west coast of Vancouver Island where the
logging practices of a large international forestry company have given
birth to the greatest civil disobedience movement in the history of
Canada. But the battle between the environmentalists and the logging
company is not the first major confrontation which has occurred there.

In June, 1811, the American ship *Tonquin*, commanded by Captain
Jonathan Thorn arrived in the sound to trade for sea otter skins with
the Native people. Something went wrong and three days later the
natives attacked the vessel, killing the captain and almost all of the
crew. The few survivors, with one exception, tried to escape in a small
boat, but that one man, Mr. Lewis, the ship's clerk, was too badly
wounded and chose to remain on board. The attackers crowded onto
the vessel and, when the decks were full of them, Lewis touched off the
barrels of gunpowder in the ship's magazine, blowing everything and
everybody to pieces. The ship's interpreter, a Native from the Astoria
area, survived to tell the tale.

Clayoquot Sound was also the place where, twenty years earlier, another
American vessel, the *Columbia*, had overwintered. In the spring of
1792, it sailed south again and its crew became the first Europeans to
discover the great river, which they named the Columbia after their
ship.

And in Clayoquot Sound lies Meares Island, named after Commander
John Meares, Royal Navy, who wrote the passage quoted above.

John Meares arrived at Nootka Sound, which is only a few miles
northwest of Clayoquot Sound, in 1788, commanding one of two
British ships trading out of the Portugese colony of Macao on the coast
of China. From the local chief, Maquinna, Meares bought some land
for eight or ten sheets of copper and some other small items and built
a storehouse on it. On June 14th of that year, he sailed down to

Clayoquot and visited the local chief there, a man whose name Meares wrote down as Wicananish. There, Meares set out for display various articles which he was offering for trade, including two copper kettles. The Natives had never seen such utensils before and immediately they were taken and placed into the chief's treasure chest a large, carved wooden box adorned with human teeth. Fifty sea otter skins were given in trade for the kettles and when these were sold back in China, the price which they fetched was the equivalent of $2,500 in the dollars of the 1790s.

So much for history. The raspberry which Commander Meares reported upon was the *Rubus parviflorus* or thimble berry, which still grows throughout our area. *Rubus* comes from the Latin word *ruber*, meaning red, which is also where the word ruby comes from. It refers to the color of the berries produced by this family of plants. *Parviflorus* means small-flowered, which seems odd when one realizes that the thimble berry flowers are much larger than those of its local relations, such as the salmonberry and the various forms of blackberries. The leaves, however, are considerably larger than those of the other plants, so the flowers do look quite small by comparison. The fruit is much like that of the cultivated raspberry in both appearance and taste and can be used in the same ways.

In his *Dyetary of Helth*, published in 1542, Andrew Boorde wrote, "All manner of wines be made of grapes except respyce, the which is made of a bery." Respyce, or raspberry wine still makes an appearance at fall fairs around our region and very good it can be too. All we need now is thimble berry wine.

SEA BLUSH or CORN SALAD

Yet the night came and she must go to bed
Beside her husband, as is oft the way,
And turning to him privately she said,
'Sweet and beloved husband, if I may,'
There is a thing I dearly wish to say....'

Geoffrey Chaucer, Second Nun's Tale

The rather nasty way in which St. Cecilia was put to death has been mentioned twice so far, so perhaps a little bit about her life might be in order. As we know, she was a Sicilian virgin. She had managed to maintain her state of chastity through prayer and fully intended to continue to do so for the rest of her life. However, as was the custom in those days, her parents arranged for her to be married off to a young man, whose name was Valerian.

When the young couple went to bed on their wedding night, Cecilia, as the poet said, turned to her husband and told him that she had a guardian angel who would kill anyone, including Valerian, who tried to defile her. The bridegroom, being a suspicious sort of chap, replied that she had better show him this angel, otherwise he would have to assume that she wasn't the virgin which she claimed to be, in which case he would kill both her and her lover.

Cecilia, therefore, sent Valerian off to visit St. Urban and ask him to get the angel to reveal himself. The angel did so, Valerian was convinced and, although they should both have lived happily ever after, they didn't. The local authorities ordered them to make sacrifices to Jupiter and they refused to do so. Valerian had his head chopped off and Cecilia went into the boiler.

And all of this, of course, is by way of introduction to the Valerian plant family. One of these, which used to be called the *Valerianella congesta*, or the little valerian with a congested flower head, had its name changed to the *Plectritis congesta*, although it is still a member of its original family group. It is one of our beautiful small spring flowers, coming into bloom in late April and early May.

162

The *Plectritis* part of the new name comes from the Greek word *plektros*, which means a plectrum or a small piece of ivory, shaped like a leaf, which musicians used to pluck the strings of instruments such as a lyre. The same sort of thing is called a guitar pick today. The leaves of this particular plant fit the description of a plectrum, so a *Plectritis* it became.

It has, however, two totally different common names. North of the border, this plant is known as a sea blush, presumably because it usually grows on grassy slopes close to the sea and its flowers are blush pink in color. South of the border, it has inherited the name of a close relative, the *Valerianella locusta*, which is called corn salad in England. So here we have, on opposite sides of Haro Strait, corn salad growing on Orcas Island while sea blush blooms on Saturna and without knowing the botanic name to confirm what one is talking about, who would know that they are one and the same plant?

St. Urban, who, at the time of Valerian's visit was merely Pope Urban I, was martyred by beheading on May 25, 230 A.D.

And as for Cecilia's husband's flower being named after a guitar pick, well, she is, after all, the patron saint of music.

SWEET BRIARS AND SNOW BERRIES

I know a bank whereon the wild thyme blows,
Where oxlips and the nodding violet grows
Quite over-canopied with luscious woodbine,
With sweet musk-roses and with eglantine.
William Shakespeare, Midsummer Night's Dream

Eglantine. *Rosa eglanteria*. Sweet briar. John Gerard wrote, "The sweet brier doth oftentimes grow higher than all the kindes of roses; ...the leaves are glittering and of a beautiful greene colour, of smell most pleasant; ...the fruit is long, of colour somewhat red, like a little olive stone. Even children with great delight eat the berries thereof when they be ripe...cookes and gentlewomen make Tarts and such like dishes for pleasure thereof, and therefore shall this suffice for the description."

Whether it was because of the useful hips or the "most pleasant" apple scent of the leaves, the sweet briar was brought to this part of the world from Europe in the nineteenth century and has become a very welcome part of our local landscape. Particularly after rain, its sweet perfume fills the air for several yards around each plant and adds to the pleasure of those who walk past, even though many may not know where the scent comes from.

The name Eglantine is probably derived from the Latin word *aculentus*, meaning prickly, for all of the briars are certainly that, being well supplied with many sharply pointed thorns. These also made them valued components of hedge rows, discouraging animals from pushing through into the farmer's fields. Their pale pink roses, opening in May and June, are similar to those of our native Nootka rose, but it is the red rose-hips, which remain on the plant after the leaves have fallen, which help to provide us with a splash of color beside our roads as winter approaches.

A second colorful berry which we see in winter is the white snow berry. This is a plant which is native to the whole of North America, but which was first really brought to the attention of Europeans as a result of the Lewis and Clark expedition of 1803-06. Seven years later, President Thomas Jefferson, who had ordered the expedition and who was a keen gardener, wrote to a friend, Madame la Comptesse de Tesse, saying, "I have growing, which I destine for you, a very handsome little shrub of the size of a currant bush. Its beauty consists in a great produce of berries of the size of currants and literally as white as snow, which remain on the bush throughout the winter, after its leaves have fallen.... We call it the Snow Berry bush, no botanical name being yet given to it."

We still call it the snow berry bush, but it now has a botanic name, *Symphoricarpus albus*, which just means, appropriately enough, clusters of white berries.

Along our road sides, the rose hips and the snow berries, with the dark green of the fir trees and salal behind them in the woods, provide us naturally with all of the colors of Christmas—of holly and ivy and mistletoe—more beautiful by far and more soothing to the soul than any of the glitz and glitter of plastic department store decorations.

QUEEN ANNE'S LACE

Sowe carrets in your garden, and humbly praise God for them
as for a singular and great blessing.

Richard Gardiner

Gardiner wrote that in his 1599 *Profitable Instructions for the Manuring, Sowing and Planting
of Kitchen Gardens*. The reason why he was so
enthusiastic about carrots was that, a few years
earlier, German horticulturalists had taken the
wild carrot, *Daucus carota*, which, as a dish, was
barely worth enthusing over, and, by selective
breeding, had come up with a significant im-
provement. For the first time, one could sow
carrot seeds in one's garden and be certain that a
fairly edible root would develop. But this new vegetable was not exactly
what we think of as a carrot today. Our present versions originated from
further breeding carried out in the 1870s by French botanists, which
led to the chantenay and nantes strains and then to the newer varieties
which we can buy in the 1990s.

But of course the wild carrot didn't die out because somebody altered
the size and taste of some of them. *Daucus carota* had been around for
a long time and is with us still. *Daucus* was its ancient Greek name and
carota was the Roman name and although it may have originated in the
dry conditions of Greece and Rome, it spread north throughout the rest
of Europe. Unfortunately, so too did some of its not-so-nice relatives.
Then, either deliberately or inadvertently, many of them, the good and
the bad, crossed the Atlantic and have become established here as well.

Certainly one of those which we could do without is the poison hemlock. In Plato's dialogue, *Phaedo*, the Greek philosopher Socrates,
sentenced to death for introducing strange gods and corrupting youth,
discusses the question of immortality of the soul with his friends during
the last hour of his life, before he drinks a draught of hemlock juice
and dies. In confirmation of the toxicity of this plant, the Roman army
doctor Dioscorides described poison hemlock as being so poisonous
that "whosoever taketh of it into his body, dieth remedieless."

Having pointed out that the wild carrot and poison hemlock are related

166

and might even be mistaken for each other by those who fail to make a proper identification, it is perhaps unkind to mention that a number of other, perfectly safe, plants which we eat regularly are also close family members and have similar appearances. These include parsley, dill, coriander and, of course, garden carrots. But since none of these are likely to be found outside the confines of a garden, probably the wisest approach is to avoid eating any of this type of plant found in the wild.

In North America, the wild carrot is known as Queen Anne's lace, a name which, in England, is applied to what we call cow parsley, another close relative. No one, however, seems to be certain as to which of the five Queen Annes is being referred to. Since the name existed before the Queen Anne who touched the young Samuel Johnson on the neck to cure his scrofula, it can't have been her. Anne of Denmark, the wife of James I, is a possibility. A historian has described her as a woman "with a long nose, a good nature and a trivial mind," but she took an interest in herbal remedies and was the queen, first of Scotland and then of England also, at the time that Gardiner wrote his comment about carrots. Anne of Cleves, the fourth wife of Henry VIII, turned out when he met her to be so unattractive to him that their marriage was never consummated. She actually referred to herself as "Your Majesty's most loyal and obedient sister." The marriage was annulled after six months, which was hardly long enough for the common people to name a plant after her. Anne Boleyn, Henry's second wife, of whom he said, "The Great Whore she is called by the people and the Great Whore she is," before he had her head chopped off, is also an unlikely source of the name, which leaves only Anne of Bohemia, the dearly loved wife of Richard II, who died in 1394 as the last possible candidate. Of them all, the good natured one would have to be my choice.

As for recognizing Queen Anne's lace, it has lacy, fernlike leaves, grows from one to three feet tall and has a mop head of tiny white flowers, each on its own little stalk, branching from the top of the main stem. One feature which distinguishes it from all its cousins and which John Gerard commented upon 400 years ago, is that there is often a single purple flower in the center of the head, among all the white ones. Nobody knows why it is there.

After the flowers die, the seeds on their stalks close in together, making a shape which gave the plant its other common name, the bird's nest.

167

BLACK MEDIC

Nec pueros coram populo Medea trucidet.

Horace, De Arte Poeticae

Nor let Medea (on the stage) slaughter her children in the sight of the audience.

There is a little annual plant which grows abundantly in grassy places throughout most of this area and which looks like a tiny yellow clover. Its common name is black medic, black because of the color of its seed pods and medic because it is very closely related to alfalfa, also known as purple medic, from its old Roman name *medica*. And the story of how it got this name brings together several of the other tales in this book.

Remember Chiron, the centaur who taught Achilles how to use yarrow to cure wounds? Well, he also had another pupil, a young fellow named Jason. At the eastern end of the Black Sea lay the kingdom of Colchis, where a fleece of pure gold from a winged ram was hung, nailed to an oak tree and guarded by a fierce dragon. In brief, Jason decided to steal it. Fortunately for him, the king of Colchis' daughter, Medea, fell for him and helped him to get it, using sorceries which she had learned from her Aunt Circe, of enchanter's nightshade fame.

When Jason and his Argonauts got home with the fleece, Medea claimed and won for him the kingdom of Corinth, where currants come from. He married her and they had two children, but shortly after that, Jason lost interest in her and divorced her in order to marry someone else. In revenge, Medea murdered the two children whom Jason had fathered and fled back to Colchis, ending up by becoming the ruler of a nearby kingdom, which was named Media after her.

168

When Nebuchadnezzar, the Hanging Gardens of Babylon builder and thrower into the burning fiery furnace of Shadrach, Meshach and Abednego, died at a great old age, his son succeeded him, but was soon killed. "And Darius the Median took the kingdom", or so it says in the Bible. Either this same Darius or one of his progeny who was called by the same name, invaded Greece in the fifth century B.C., taking with him from Media the seeds of the alfalfa plant, which grew wild in his home kingdom, in order to plant fodder for his horses or possibly to use as a herbal remedy, because weight for weight, alfalfa contains four times as much vitamin C as does orange juice. That's one reason why alfalfa sprouts are so popular today.

Four centuries later, the Roman legions under the command of Julius Caesar overran the kingdom of Pontus on the shore of the Black Sea, just to the west of Media. That was where Caesar came up with his "Veni, vidi, vici" comment. His army doctor at the time was the Greek born Dioscorides, whom we've met several times already and was the chap who recommended bluebell juice as a hair remover. He looted Cratevas' drawings of plants from Pontus and incorporated them into his famous book when he retired from the military.

In that book, he called the plant which Darius had brought into Greece medike, after Media, the country where it had originated. Dioscorides was writing in Greek, but when his work was later translated into Latin, a language where the letter K hardly exists, the name of the plant became medica and the title of the book became *De Materia Medica*.

Whether Medea, through the plant which was almost directly named after her, also gave us, from the same source, our modern words medical, medicine and so on, or it is all just some most remarkable coincidence, one can only guess. But whenever you take your medicine or eat alfalfa sprouts or see the little yellow flowers in the grass, perhaps you'll think of Medea. And certainly, if you perform her story on the stage, either in the form of Euripides' drama or Cherubini's opera, you'll remember what Horace advised, won't you?

THORNY DANDELIONS?

Every bird is known by its feathers.

Dr. Thomas Fuller, Gnomologia

A nature column in an English Sunday newspaper told about a lady who only knew the names of two birds, which she called the robin red-breast and the Jenny wren. She then referred to all other birds by one of these two names, altered slightly according to the color of their feathers. To her, for example, a goldfinch would be a yellow Jenny wren and a blackbird, a black robin red-breast.

A well known Canadian bird expert has another system. He refers to any bird which he is not sure about as either an LBB (Little Brown Bird) or an LCC (Little Colorful Critter).

Both of these approaches have their merits. One of these is that they avoid passing false identifications to other people. They might not, perhaps, be totally acceptable at the annual bird count: "I saw 64 LBBs, 39 LCCs and 2 black and white robin red-breasts swimming in the bay," but for everyday purposes, there's not too much wrong with them.

One can even use the same approach with wildflowers. For instance, it wouldn't be too difficult to recognize a chicory flower if it was described as a blue dandelion, which is exactly what it does look like, or a Douglas aster which was referred to as a tall, pale lavender daisy.

Beside the road near our home, several different yellow flowers bloom each summer. At first glance, many of them look a bit like dandelions, which are flowers that almost everyone can recognize, and if one were to describe the ditches as being full of dandelions, one wouldn't be giving too false an impression. The fact that, except in spring, there are no real dandelions there is fairly immaterial. What grows there in summer are hawksbeards and hairy cats' ears, Chilean tarweed and large-leaved avens and adding to the general sense of yellowness, wall lettuce, nipplewort, buttercups and even a yellow rose.

The poet Swinburne described Eton College as being "Bright with names that men remember, loud with names that men forget." That could just as well apply to all of our roadside ditches, wherever we happen to live.

So if anyone wants to talk of the yellow rose as a "big, thorny dandelion bush," who are we to quibble?

> For Lo, the winter is past, the rain is over and gone, the flowers appear on the earth, the time of the singing of birds has come.
> *The Song of Solomon*

A Guide To Collecting
Wild Herbs

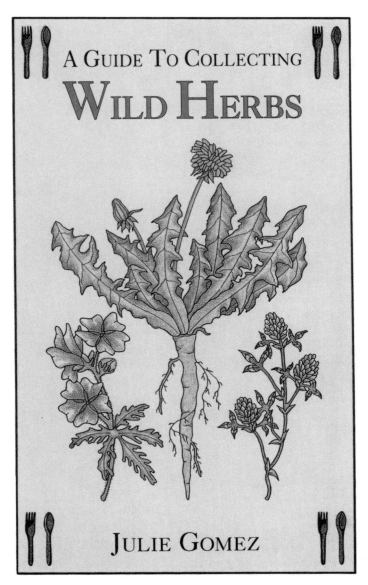

Julie Gomez

Julie Gomez
5 1/2 x 8 1/2, 64 pp., SC   ISBN 0-88839-390-3

Available from Hancock House Publishers, 19313 Zero Ave., Surrey, B.C. V4P 1M7
1-800-938-1114 Fax (604) 538-2262   1431 Harrison Ave., Blaine, WA 98230

Wildflowers of the West

Mabel Crittenden
5 1/2 x 8 1/2, 206 pp., SC   ISBN 0-88839-270-2

Available from Hancock House Publishers, 19313 Zero Ave., Surrey, B.C. V4P 1M7
1-800-938-1114 Fax (604) 538-2262   1431 Harrison Ave., Blaine, WA 98230

MORE GREAT HANCOCK HOUSE TITLES

Outdoor Titles

12 Basic Skills of Flyfishing
Ted Peck & Ed Rychkun
ISBN 0-88839-392-X

Adventure with Eagles
David Hancock
ISBN 0-88839-217-6

Alpine Wildflowers
Ted Underhill
ISBN 0-88839-975-8

Birds of North America
David Hancock
ISBN 0-88839-220-6

Coastal Lowland Flowers
Ted Underhill
ISBN 0-88839-973-1

Eastern Rocks & Minerals
James Grandy
ISBN 0-88839-105-6

Eastern Mushrooms
Barrie Kavasch
ISBN 0-88839-091-2

Edible Seashore
Rick Harbo
ISBN 0-88839-199-4

Guide to Collecting Wild Herbs
Julie Gomez
ISBN 0-88839-390-3

Northeastern Wild Edibles
Barrie Kavasch
ISBN 0-88839-090-4

Orchids of North America
Dr. William Petrie
ISBN 0-88839-089-0

Pacific Wilderness
Hancock, Hancock & Sterling
ISBN 0-919654-08-8

Roadside Wildflowers NW
Ted Underhill
ISBN 0-88839-108-0

Sagebrush Wildflowers
Ted Underhill
ISBN 0-88839-171-4

Seashells of the Northeast Coast
Gordon & Weeks
ISBN 0-88839-808-7

Tidepool & Reef
Rick Harbo
ISBN 0-88839-039-4

Trees of the West
Mabel Crittenden
ISBN 0-88839-269-9

Upland Field and Forest Wildflowers
Ted Underhill
ISBN 0-88839-171-4

Western Mushrooms
Ted Underhill
ISBN 0-88839-031-9

Wildflowers of the West
Mabel Crittenden
ISBN 0-88839-270-2

Wild Harvest
Terry Domico
ISBN 0-88839-022-X

Wildlife of the Rockies
Hancock & Hall
ISBN 0-919654-33-9